MW01032489

Witchcraft

What You Need to Know About Witchcraft, Wicca, and Paganism, Including Wiccan Beliefs, White Magic Spells, and Rituals

© Copyright 2019

All Rights Reserved. No part of this book may be reproduced in any form without permission in writing from the author. Reviewers may quote brief passages in reviews.

Disclaimer: No part of this publication may be reproduced or transmitted in any form or by any means, mechanical or electronic, including photocopying or recording, or by any information storage and retrieval system, or transmitted by email without permission in writing from the publisher.

While all attempts have been made to verify the information provided in this publication, neither the author nor the publisher assumes any responsibility for errors, omissions or contrary interpretations of the subject matter herein.

This book is for entertainment purposes only. The views expressed are those of the author alone, and should not be taken as expert instruction or commands. The reader is responsible for his or her own actions.

Adherence to all applicable laws and regulations, including international, federal, state and local laws governing professional licensing, business practices, advertising and all other aspects of doing business in the US, Canada, UK or any other jurisdiction is the sole responsibility of the purchaser or reader.

Neither the author nor the publisher assumes any responsibility or liability whatsoever on the behalf of the purchaser or reader of these materials. Any perceived slight of any individual or organization is purely unintentional.

Contents

Introduction

To start, there is a quick introduction to the concepts of witchcraft, Wicca, and Paganism. These are the main topics of the book, so it is important that you have a bit of an understanding of them before diving in.

Then the topic of witchcraft is explored. This will cover what it is and what it involves. You will learn that witchcraft isn't a religion but simply something that religion can choose to do.

The content next focuses on Wicca. This is probably one of the most popular Pagan religions of the day. Just remember: this is not the only Pagan path you have to choose from, but if it resonates with you, then so be it.

After this is Paganism, an umbrella term for pretty much any religion that doesn't fall under the regular mainstream religions of Christianity, Judaism, and so on. This will also provide you with other religions that you could choose to follow instead of Wicca, and which will often use witchcraft as well. That being said, you do not have to choose a specific Pagan religion to be Pagan and practice witchcraft. There is an all-inclusive sect called "Eclectic Paganism" that many Pagans say they belong to.

The book then looks at white magic spells. These are all good spells that are easy for beginners to use and work very well in any Pagan religion. They involve things like plants, herbs, crystals, and even a relaxing bath.

Next is rituals. Rituals play a very big part in Pagan religions because Pagans love to celebrate. This is great, though, because rituals are usually followed by a delicious meal to share with family and friends.

Lastly, you will find another section for spells. This will be full of spells to help every area of your life, including love, wealth, health, careers, healing, travel, and fertility.

Introduction to Witchcraft, Wicca, and Paganism

Pictures of witches have been seen in many different forms throughout history. They have been ugly hags with warts on their nose huddled over cauldrons of bubbly liquids to evil, cackling beings flying around on brooms in pointy hats. Pop culture has made witches a benevolent housewife to an awkward teenager and even a charmed trio of sisters battling evil. However, the true history of witches is a bit darker—and deadlier.

Witches are people who practice witchcraft. They use magic to call upon spirits in order to bring about change or ask them for help. After Christianity started to take hold of the masses, witches were often viewed as Pagans doing the work of the Devil. Most of them, though, were natural healers, or what would have been called "wise women" whose profession was misunderstood by most.

It is unknown when witches first appeared, but they were around long before mainstream religions started to take control and change the way people lived. During the early centuries of human life, witches were the women who spoke with the goddesses and were revered. The ancient civilizations of the Middle East worshipped powerful female deities, but women were the ones who typically practiced the most important rituals. These trained priestesses were known as wise women, and are likely the earliest forms of women who became known as witches.

People called on these women like doctors, and they would make house calls, help with infertility, deliver babies, and cure impotence. So why did these women get transformed into the malevolent beings that so many people see when they hear the word "witch" or "witchcraft"?

While most people believe Christianity is to blame, there could be a link to events long before Christ entered the scene. Indo-Europeans started expanding westward, and with them, they brought the warrior culture that saw aggression as important, and they worshipped male gods of war, which would dominate the female deities.

Others blame the Hebrews, who settled in, and their monotheistic, male-centric view of creation. The Hebrews, who obeyed the laws of the *Bible*, viewed witchcraft as something dangerous, and they prohibited those Pagan practices.

Centuries after, this fear of witches started to move through Europe like wildfire. When the plague decimated Europe in the 1300s and killed most of the population, it also created hysteria. Amid all of this, many people blamed the Devil as the reason for their misfortune. The Catholic Church, which had been established for a few decades at this point, started to grow its efforts to punish non-Catholic causes of mass death, which would include the "devil-doting" witches.

They believed that these women worshipped in nocturnal assemblies, where they would perform various social ills, like gluttonous feasting on human babies, naked dancing, and sex. People of this time thought that the Devil would make an appearance at these "festivals" and participate in the orgy.

So, they thought they needed to "tame" these women to keep everybody else safe. This led Henrik Kramer and Jacob Springer to write the *Malleus Maleficarum* (the *Hammer of Witches*), which was meant to help witch hunters diagnose and punish these witches. This witch-hunting hysteria would peak in the 1600s. The worst happened in Germany and France. In Wurzburg, Germany, the magistrates ruled that the majority of the town had been possessed by the Devil, and condemned hundreds of people to die. Some towns in Germany were left without women.

Thousands of women were arrested and taken to inquisitors. They stripped and searched them, looking for any "suspicious" birthmark, wart, or mole. If any was found, they were sentenced to death. However, the women had to confess before they could be executed, so torture seemed to be the best way to go. The Church used things like thumb and leg screws, the iron maiden, and head clamps to draw the "truth" from these women that they needed to enact death.

Once these things stopped around the eighteenth century, around 60,000 people in Europe had been murdered as witches. In the Americas, the most famous witch hunt took place in Salem, Massachusetts. This area had already undergone some rough times with war, land disputes, and religious divisions.

The Salem Witch Trials began with two girls playing a simple game and then spread the town until nine girls were "stricken" with an "ailment" and the jails were filled with over 200 witches. It spread out to 24 other villages, and of those jailed, 27 were found guilty, and nineteen of them killed.

The trails came to a quick end because the "victims" started to point their fingers at important people in the community. When the governor of Massachusetts's wife was accused of being a witch, leaders saw to it that everything ended quickly. Centuries after this took place, it is a belief that social release was the cause of the Witch Trials. The girls were so controlled in Salem that the confessions gave them a chance to get attention.

Fortunately, in today's time, this fearsome image of the witch has faded away. And even though the witch hunts targeted women, men were, and can still be, witches. Unfortunately, for women, they have been and are still seen as the weaker sex, so that makes them "vulnerable".

Paganism and witchcraft were never eradicated from the world like the witch hunts tried to do. Practitioners got smarter and learned how to hide their practices during the ups and downs of witchcraft over the years. There have also been many different types of Paganism—many of which you will learn about later on. Shamanism is probably the oldest Pagan practice. Shamans practiced magic and would perform dreamwork and go into meditative trances.

In Ancient Babylon and Samaria, they created what is known as Demonology. They believed that there were spirits everywhere, and most were hostile. They thought that people needed to use magic in order to protect themselves from these hostile spirits. Most of today's beliefs have been drawn from the beliefs of the Ancient Romans, Greeks, Hebrews, Egyptians, and Celts. The Celtic beliefs are probably the most popular Pagan belief system. Most Pagan belief systems are considered a nature religion, and this is because Celts loved their land and used the land's natural resources to survive.

These various Pagan belief systems make it much easier for people today to start following a Pagan path. It can also make it frustrating to figure out what you should and shouldn't do. However, the most important thing you should do, if you want to follow a Pagan path, is to blaze your own. If one particular belief system resonates with you, then follow it. Learn its beliefs and rules and go for it. If there are many belief systems in your life, then take bits and pieces of each and walk your own eclectic path. As long as it feels right, then it is right for you.

This is kind of how Wicca came to be, and why there are so many offshoots of Wicca. Wicca is the newest Pagan religion, having only been founded in 1954 by Gerald Gardner. The chapter on Wicca goes in-depth on how it came to be, but it is believed to have roots in European Pagan faiths. This is just one example of how open Paganism is for people. You have the freedom of having many gods and goddesses you worship, or you can simply have a Universal power. That's why there is a whole group of people who refer to themselves as eclectic Pagans.

While most countries do not have witch trials anymore, there are still plenty of people who don't understand Paganism and witchcraft. Mainstream religions still teach that witches are bad people, so there is a stigma, but that shouldn't discourage from following your heart. You know you aren't doing the Devil's work. You know that you aren't harming anybody, so do as you will. However, while on the topic of the Devil, there are some rumors about Paganism, witchcraft, and the Devil that should be dispelled.

As mentioned, the Catholic Church, along with Hebrews and other Christian religions, said that witches were working for the Devil, but where did "the Devil" really come from?

The Devil, or Satan, is a being within Abrahamic religions that makes humans do sinful acts and lie. The Pagans who lived before the religions were formed did not have "a devil" or Satan, nor did they believe in Heaven or Hell. So, this idea of Satan does not play a role in Pagan belief systems. That said, there are two types of Satanists, which would technically be Pagan religions. One type of Satanist following, known as LaVeyan Satanism, has Satan as simply a symbol of liberty. These Satanists are actually atheists and do not worship any type of deity. The other type of Satanists, known as Theistic Satanism, have Satan as a deity that they revere and worship. These belief systems—that do fall under Pagan religion—will not be explored, though, as this book's focus is on Paganism being a nature religion, and neither of these other systems teaches things about witchcraft and honoring Mother Nature for what She brings us.

Back to Satan, the *Bible* never explicitly mentions the Devil or Satan. Instead, this idea of a fallen angel hell-bent on wreaking havoc on Earth was created to elicit fear among the follows of the Christian faith. This was one of many tactics that Abrahamic religions used to try and convince people of Ancient Pagan faiths to switch to these new religions.

Making people fear this evil being, and fear going to hell when they died, was simply a way to keep followers in-line. As far as tactics to take over the religious scene, Abrahamic religions also started to take over Pagan festivals. The most popular example of this is when the Christian leaders changed the Yule festival into a birthday celebration for Jesus. Doing this made it easier for them to get Pagans to convert to Christianity. Many other examples of this are provided throughout the book.

As you can see, Paganism and witchcraft have pretty interesting roots. From witch hunts to conversions, it is amazing that these old-nature religions have survived the years. However, thanks to ancestors who were not willing to be scared into changing, people have knowledge and understanding of these belief systems and gives them the chance to carry them forward. Hopefully, one day, Pagans can freely practice without worrying about meeting people who condemn them to an eternal life of hellfire and damnation.

Witchcraft

For a simple definition, witchcraft is the magical manipulation of energy to change something. The energy that the witch uses can be stones, herbs, environmental, or any other natural object. It could simply be from the witch or channeled through the God or Goddess. Many witches will cast spells that incorporate all of these in ritual practice. However, one doesn't have to engage in rituals or cast spells to do something magical or be considered a witch.

Witchcraft is made up of a spiritual system that respects a person's free will and the thoughts of the person, and it encourages people to understand and learn Nature and Earth, which helps to affirm the divinity of things. The most important thing is that it teaches responsibility. People have to accept responsibility for their actions because whatever happens is a result of them. People cannot blame some exterior force or being for their mistakes, weaknesses, or shortcomings. If they end up messing something up or acting in a way that hurts someone, they can blame no one but themselves and will have to face the consequences.

The spells that can be performed in witchcraft will often involve things like wisdom, harmony, creativity, healing, and love. The potions that are stirred could be to remedy a headache, relieve a cold, or a herbal dip to get rid of fleas on cats. People might want to learn more and use Nature's remedies as much as they can instead of solely relying on synthetic drugs.

Many women and men label themselves as witches and practice witchcraft today. The type of witchcraft that they practice varies widely and can be spiritual expressions for several different religions. As odd as it might sound, there are even atheist witches.

Witchcraft can take on several different forms. Some people choose to cast a circle each month on the Full Moon, New Moon, or both. Some will plan their spells carefully based on the planets, Sun, and Moon. Some will simply cast spells when they are the most convenient. The spell's nature could vary. Some people will cast circles and do a full ritual each time, but others will sometimes settle in, focus all their energy, and then send it out into the Universe. Many modern witches will make protection charms for themselves, their cars, pets, family, and homes. They may also create herbal combinations for healing and other users, and they will sometimes cast spells if they have the time and space.

Witches have, especially those of the Wiccan faith, follow a Law of Three, which means that whatever you send out will return to the sender three-fold, whether good or bad. Witches will hesitate before performing magic that could manipulate or harm other people because it could boomerang back to them much larger and harder than they sent it out.

This by no means is saying that Witches are perfect beings; they are humans and thus make mistakes and errors in judgment. Most witches try to look at all possible outcomes of their actions and thoughts so that they can think about the serious consequences that could come back to them.

Magic

Magic, which you might have seen spelled as "magick" in some texts, is the method of controlling energy to change events or bring about some positive benefits.

Ceremonial or ritual magic is often characterized by several different elaborate, long, and complex ceremonies or rituals and involves a variety of different tools to help the practitioner.

In Ancient Hindu, sacred texts, such as the Vedas, talk about white and black magic. They also talk about mundane and supernatural magic, which is still common throughout India. In ancient practices, these "magicians" were often a special class of priests, the Magi of Zoroastrianism, and had a reputation. Along with this was the Ancient Egyptians that shaped the hermeticism of the Hellenistic religion as well as the Greek mystery religions. Then a distinction started to develop between the "high" magic of the ritual-based Theurgy and the "low" magic of the Goetia.

Tools

Tools are not a strict requirement for witchcraft; however, given the work that you are doing, these tools can be very helpful. Many are used for the same reasons, so owning them all would be redundant.

1. Besom

This is the witch's broom, which symbolizes the union of the God and Goddess. The shape is associated with masculinity, and then the three-part design shows the three cycles of femininity. This is used to cleanse your space before spell work and rituals. You do this by sweeping in a clockwise direction. Once done, open the door closest to you and sweep all of the negativity outside. The broom should be consecrated before you begin to use it, and don't use it for regular cleansing, but only for rituals. A broom hung over your door will keep out negative influences. It is also a big part of Pagan weddings. Newlyweds will often jump over the besom to attract harmony, fertility, and prosperity.

2. Athame

An athame is a double-edged blade that is used to cast a circle. Traditionally, it has a black handle. It should not be sharp because it isn't meant to cut things, but it can be used to carve sigils into candles or runes.

3. Offering Bowl

This is a great addition to a devotional shrine. It is simply a container where you place offerings for your chosen deities. You can use the same one for all of them, or you can have a different bowl for each.

4. Boline

This is a sickle that has a blade shaped like a half-moon. The handle is normally white. This is often used to harvest herbs, branches, and flowers. Many witches simply use mundane knives instead.

5. Crystals

Crystals tend to play a large role in a witch's practice. They aren't simply rocks; each crystal has its own vibrations and can help with many different things.

6. Grimoire

This is also called the Book of Shadows and is a book that holds your religious text, spells, and rituals. Many witches will use this as a journal of their practices as well.

7. Essential Oils and Herbs

Much like crystals, these things hold their own associations. Herbal magic is even its own branch of witchcraft.

8. Candles

Candles are a must-have because they play a big role in witchcraft. You can also find some for cheap, too. They can be used in a variety of ways in your rituals and spell work. Some believe that you should use a snuffer to snuff out the candle rather than blowing out the candle.

9. Chalice

This is a representation of the Goddess' womb. It is associated solely with water. Adding water to your cup can be used to represent water in your circle.

10. Cauldron

The cauldron is also symbolic of the Goddess' womb. For people who follow Celtic traditions, it represents Cerridwen, the Celtic goddess who is always stirring an elixir of knowledge. You can use it to bring water or fire into your practice. If you get a cast-iron cauldron, you can burn things in it.

These are just ten of the many different tools that witches use during their practice. The important thing is to figure out what you feel you should use and begin there. In the end, the witch is the most important tool.

The Elements

Within the Wiccan faith, everything works with the five elements: Spirit, Earth, Air, Fire, and Water. They use the symbols of these elements for spells and protections. All of the elements are connected to every single process in nature. They are also symbolic of emotional, spiritual, and physical attributes. Every practitioner should learn and feel these elements. It will take some time and effort to understand the elements. When you have read about each of these elements, try to see and feel them around you. Many Wiccans choose to meditate on the elements.

• **Spirit**

This is sometimes called Aether. It is the prime element that is present in everything. It gives connection, provides balance, and space for all the Elements to exist in. Spirit is immaterial, unlike Earth, Fire, Water, and Air. Spirit is people's sense of connectedness with wellbeing and Spirit. Spirit represents the sense of union and joy.

Most of Spirit's attributes are universal. Its symbols are rope and cord. It has the upper space on the pentagram. Its goddess is The Lady, and its god is The Horned God. It represents eternity and the wheel of the year. Its color is white, and its animal is the dove.

• **Earth**

Earth is representative of femininity, wealth, prosperity, stability, abundance, and strength. During rituals, Earth is often represented in the form of making images out of stone or wood, herbalism, and burying objects in the earth.

Earth is feminine. Its direction is North. It is receptive energy. Earth symbols include soil, clay, rocks, caves, fields, and salt. It is the lower left of a pentagram.

Earth goddesses are: Demeter, Rhea, Ceres, Gaea, Persephone, Mah, and Nephtys.

Earth gods are: Cernunnos, Tammuz, Adonis, Dionysus, Pan, Athos, Marduk, and Arawn.

Earth Spirits are: dwarfs, trolls, and gnomes.

Earth's time of day is midnight and nighttime. It represents the age part of life. Earth's season is winter. Its associated colors are yellow, green, black, and brown. Earth Zodiac signs are Virgo, Capricorn, and Taurus. It is associated with the sense of touch.

Earth crystals are: emerald, quartz, rock crystal, amethyst, onyx, azurite, jasper, and salt.

Magic tools for Earth are: stones, cords, the pentacle, gems, the pentagram, images, and salt.

Herbs, plants, and metals associated with Earth are: lichens, lilac, iron, jasmine, lead, honeysuckle, ivy, cypress, grains, patchouli, oats, and rice.

Earth animals are: dogs, ants, cows, wolves, bulls, horses, and bears.

Types of magic associated with Earth are: grounding, runes, gardening, finding treasures, magnet images, money spells, stones, binding, and knots.

Earth ritual actions are: making clay effigies, planting herbs, burying things, and planting trees.

- **Water**

Water is representative of the emotional aspects of femininity and love, the soul, eternal movement, absorption, wisdom, emotions, purification, absorption, and subconscious. During rituals, Water is represented by tossing things into water, healing spells, ritual bathing, pouring water over things, and brew making.

Water is feminine. Its direction is West. It has receptive energy. Its symbols include rain, the cup, the ocean, fog, the river, the well, the shell, spring, and the lake. It is located at the upper right on a pentagram.

Water goddesses are: Marianne, Yamaha, Aphrodite, Tiamat, Isis, and Mari.

Water gods are: Ea, Poseidon, Dylan, Neptune, Manannan, and Osiris.

Water Spirits are: nymphs, fairies of lakes, ponds, or streams, mermaids, and undines.

The time of day for Water is twilight and dusk. It represents the mature phase of life. Its season is autumn. The colors associated with Water are green, black, turquoise, blue, indigo, green, and gray. Water Zodiac signs are Scorpio, Cancer, and Pisces. The associated sense is taste.

Crystals associated with Water are: coral, aquamarine, fluorite, amethyst, blue topaz, pearl, and blue tourmaline.

Water magical tools are: goblet, mirror, cup, and cauldron.

Herbs, plants, and metals associated with Water are: bushes, willow, mercury, rose, silver, elm, copper, elder, ferns, cherry, lotus, birch, mosses, apricot, water, apple, lilies, and gardenia.

Water animals include: dragons, crabs, water snakes, turtles, dolphins, frogs, fish, and cats.

The most common types of Water magic are: mirror divination, protection spells, magnet work, cleansing, love magic, and lucid dreaming.

Ritual actions using Water are: bathing, cold herbal infusions, dilution, sprinkling, and washing.

- **Fire**

Fire is representative of love, passion, energy, leadership, and inspiration. During rituals, Fire is most often represented by the lighting of fires and candles, love spells, baking, and burning objects. Fire is the element of change. It is the representation of magic itself. Fire is the most spiritual and physical of all of the elements.

Fire is masculine. Its direction is South. It is projective energy. It is located on the lower right of the pentagram.

Symbols of fire are: the rainbow, heat, the flame, lava, lightning, stars, heated objects, the sun, and the volcano.

Fire goddesses are: Hestia, Vesta, Brigit, and Pele.

Fire gods are: Horus, Vulcan, Agni, and Prometheus.

Fire Spirits are: salamanders and firedrakes.

The time of day associated with Fire is noon. It represents the youthful part of life. Its season is summer. Colors for Fire are crimson, white, red, orange, and gold. Fire Zodiac signs are Leo, Sagittarius, and Aries. The associated sense is sight.

Fire crystals are: fire opal, agate, rube, and volcanic lava.

Magical tools that represent Fire are: herb burning, the knife, the dagger, incense, paper requests, the sword, candles, athame, the lamp, and the censer.

Plants, herbs, and metals associated with Fire are: garlic, walnut, gold, rowan, brass, holly, hibiscus, oak, red peppers, mahogany, cinnamon, juniper, coffee, fig, beans, chestnut, seeds, cedar, chili peppers, cashew, alder, and ash.

Fire animals are: bee, scorpion, fox, dragon, coyote, cat, phoenix, lion, ladybug, horse, mantis, snake, and cricket.

The most common types of Fire magic are: healing, energy work, candles, and love spells.

The most common ritual use for Fire is: heating, burning paper, objects, and wood, preparing a decoction, and cauldron work.

- **Air**

The Air is representative of intelligence and the mind, as well as wishes, dreams, knowledge, ideas, imagination, inspiration, psychic powers, and telepathy. In rituals, Air is most often represented through hiding things high up, songs, aromatherapy, and tossing things into the wind. It is the ruler of spells for finding lost items, knowledge, freedom, instruction, travel, and can help develop psychic faculties. Air is often used in visualizations.

The gender of Air is masculine. The direction of Air is East. It has projective energy. On the pentagram, it is placed in the upper left.

The most common symbols of Air are: herbs, flowers, smoke, trees, plants, sky, breath, wind, vibration, breezes, clouds, and feathers.

Air goddesses are: Cardea, Urania, Aradia, Nuit, and Arianrhod.

Air gods are: Merawrim, Knlil, Thoth, Kheoheva, and Shu.

Air Spirits are: sylphs, fairies of the trees, flowers, and winds, and zephyrs.

The time of day for Air is dawn. It represents the infancy stage of life. Its season is spring. Air colors are yellow, crimson, and white. Air Zodiac signs are Libra, Aquarius, and Gemini. The senses include hearing and smell.

The best crystals to use when working with Air are: clear quartz, alexandrite, topaz, amethyst, rainbow stones, and pumice

Magical tools associated with Air are: the wand, the sword, and the censer.

The best plants, metals, and herbs are: lavender, acacia, pine, almond, clove, maple, tin, dill, linden, copper, hazel, pansy, aspen, myrrh, primrose, and vervain.

Air animals are: raven, spider, and eagle

The type of magic most often worked with Air is: karma work, prophecy, wind magic, divination, and concentration.

Ritual actions to evoke Air are: hanging things in trees, tossing things into the air, burning incense, and playing the flute.

Circle and Altar

Something that is found in various religious traditions is an altar, which is basically a physical place that serves as a location to honor ancestors, spirits, or deities, to keep sacred things safe, and to make offerings. In Wicca, the main purpose of an altar is to act as a focal point for ritual celebrations. However, you can use an altar at other times, too, like during prayer, spell work, or meditation.

Since Wicca is most often practiced inside, sometimes outside, the Wiccan altar is usually tucked into a corner of a room and then pulled out into the center when a circle is cast during a ritual. The tools for your rituals can reside on your altar at all times, or you can store them someplace when you aren't using them.

The tools for a ritual are symbolic items that represent different parts of Nature that contribute to circumstances of life, which include the Elements, directions, and the God and Goddess. The tools will vary between the traditions, but will most often include statues or some type of representation of the God and Goddess, candles, a chalice, a wand, an athame, a bowl of salt, soil or sand, a dish of water, and a bell.

The altar can take on many different forms. Depending on what your circumstances are, it can be a permanent part of the home, or it could be a place that performs "double duty" in your home. The main requirement is that you have it on a flat surface. Many people like using a round shape that makes it easier to move inside the circle, but they don't have to be. Ideally, your altar should be a natural material like wood or stone. Wood is traditionally and typically easier to come by.

You might not have the luxury to purchase something new just to have as an altar. Don't worry—you can also place temporary altars on a coffee table or something else. You can also find some "Wiccan altar kits" online. Any type of physical object that has been charged with magical energy will provide power to your work, but the more natural it is, the more powerful it will be. Do your best to keep from working with synthetics or plastics. If you can hold a ritual outside, try using a tree stump or large rock as your altar.

If you can keep a permanent altar in your house, you can decorate the altar with colored fabrics for the season. When doing this, choose colors and items most closely associated with the seasons, like evergreens and holly berries for Yule, or flowers for spring. You can also place on it images of your deities, and your favorite stones and crystals. Just make sure you leave enough room for the tools you need to use.

As for where things should be placed, there are different layouts you can choose. These vary based on traditions, but there are some commonalities. One layout divides the altar in half. The tools for the Goddess, Earth, and Water are placed on the left. The tools for the God, Fire, and Air go on the right. Another option is to place the God and Goddess in the center of the altar with all of the tools arranged around them based on the directions and Elements. The tools for Earth will face North. The tools for Fire will face South. The tools for Air will face East. The tools for Water will face West.

Even though some follow established patterns closely, there are others called eclectics who work on intuition. They use patterns that resonate with their own experiences of the symbols, deities, and tools. Some like to be elaborate in their setup, while others will take a subtler approach. Space will also play a huge factor.

For many beginners, the first time they set up their altar could be very daunting. Depending on the things that you have read, it might seem like you could make a mistake, or you might feel like you are not completely following the rules if you don't have everything exactly right. If you begin to feel like this, this would be a good time to remind yourself that the Goddess and God aren't concerned about the quality or size of your altar or how many candles are on it. The most important thing is to work with what you have. Your altar will evolve with your practice.

As mentioned in this section, the altar is the center point of your ritual circles. Circle-casting is one of the main skills that Wiccans need when practicing witchcraft. It is normally the first thing that you will learn how to do. It is a complex idea, but the techniques are simple.

Circle-casting is the practice of creating a temporary spot for rituals or magic. It is round, obviously. This circle is a mobile temple and is a place separate from the ordinary world where your magic works better.

Generally, circles are cast at the beginning of a ritual by the leader of the coven, but solo practitioners will cast circles, too. When the ritual ends, the circle gets released. The circle acts as a psychic boundary. While you cannot feel it with your regular five senses, a properly cast circle can be felt through your energy or clairvoyance by a person who has these skills.

Casting a circle is not necessarily a requirement, but it helps to shut off any disruptive influences so that you can stay focused on your work. If you ever perform magical trances, it can be very psychically vulnerable, so witches will often cast circles as psychic protection.

Not only is the outer barrier important, but so is its inner one. Magical energy bounces around and scatters throughout the Universe. It is naturally in motion. The point of having a ritual is to concentrate that energy temporarily for a certain purpose. The circle gives you the chance to gather more energy and hold on to it. If you are evoking spirits or deities, a circle gives them a place to land.

This could be summarized by saying there are two main purposes for a circle: to keep things out and to keep energy in.

The circle has been described as a bubble, fence, vessel, gate, workbench, and several other metaphors. All of these can describe the circle, but none of them really explain what it is.

For a solo practitioner, it is normally around five to six feet in diameter, but this can grow bigger if the group is fairly large. The circle can be physically defined by candles or scarves, or it can be marked by placing symbolic items at the four cardinal points.

There are different ways that a circle can be cast. The following is a simple way to cast a simple circle. This is a great place to start, and then you can adapt and change it as your practice changes and grows:

1. Find a place that is open and flat where you won't be bothered.

2. With a compass, find the four cardinal points—you can probably find an app for this on your phone.

3. Put something that is representative of each of the elements at each of the points around your imaginary circle so that the circle is about five to six feet in diameter. This means that if you stand in the middle, facing North, your Earth element should be placed about three feet in front of you.

   a. **Water is West** – sea shell or chalice with water

   b. **Fire is South** – candle, essential oil burner with tea light

   c. **Air is East** – feather, incense with holder, or sage

   d. **Earth is North** – rocks, crystals, potted plant, or ceramic dish

4. Face East while standing in the center of the circle. Relax and take a few deep breaths until you feel present, centered, and calm. Visualize the wind whipping around you and begin to really feel the air. Chant: "Spirits of Air, I call on you."

Then face South. Imagine a warm fire and the sun at noon. Really feel yourself connected to the Fire and chant: "Spirits of Fire, I call on you."

Face West and visualize water rushing through the streams and waves. When you feel connected to Water, chant: "Spirits of Water, I call on you."

Face North and get the scent of how the earth smells after it has rained. Visualize the darkness of a cave and being rooted to the earth from your feet. When you feel connected, chant: "Spirits of Earth, I call on you."

Remain turned toward the North and begin to notice your feet. Allow them to shoot roots down and connect with the Earth's core. Allow a golden white light to travel up from the Earth's center and through your body. Chant: "Mother Earth, I call on you."

Now, send light up from the crown of your head and into the atmosphere to connect you with the Infinite Cosmos. Pull white light down into and through you. Chant: "Father Sky, I call on you."

Feel yourself contained and protected on every side, as well as below and above. Feel grateful for the Divine support. Chant: "Thank you, thank you, thank you. The circle is cast. Blessed be."

5. Now, you can either sit or stand inside the circle and do your magic or meditate.

6. After you have finished, you have to close the circle and thank the cosmos. To close the circle, stand and face West. Visualize Water again and say: "Water, you were here, and I thank you."

Turn toward the South and think about Fire and say: "Fire, you were here, and I thank you."

Turn toward the East and think about Earth and say: "Earth, you were here, and I thank you."

Turn toward the North and think about Mother Earth and say: "Mother Earth, you were here, and I thank you."

Think about Father Sky again, and say: "Father Sky, you were here, and I thank you."

Say: "Thank you, thank you, thank you. Blessed be. And so, it is."

Take a few minutes and say: "The circle is open, but never broken. The love of the Goddess is forever in my heart. Merry meet, and merry part and merry meet again."

Really visualize, feel, and sense all of the energy you have raised being released back into the Universe. Trust that it is going to work, and truly know that your magic is complete.

Book of Shadows

It really doesn't matter what you call it; a Book of Shadows, Book of Magic, or a Magical Grimoire, every witch needs to keep a personal record of their work. These are great places where you can keep your personal notes and a little diary of your magical experiences. This is where you can write down your dreams, aspiration, interpretations, and affirmations. A simple definition of it would be a book that a witch keeps and uses to write down their research, spiritual information, experiences, and thoughts, along with incantations, spells, and potions.

Origins

As with a spiritual text out there, there is a big debate as to when and how the Book of Shadows came to be. Some think that they were popular during the Middle Ages and were written in Runic alphabets in order to hide their meanings. Some people say that the witches of the Middle Ages were illiterate, and these books weren't written until the fourteenth and fifteenth centuries. Even during this time, they would have used the Runic alphabet to protect themselves from persecution and even death.

It does not matter how they got their start; they have been given several different names. The most famous mythological type of these books is called *The Golden Grimoire*, which is thought to be Merlin the Magician's Book of Shadows.

Inside the early Books of Shadows of the 1950s and 60s, there were not many rituals. They included things such as history and an overview of the belief system of the witches that used them. Occasionally, some of these books contained a small ritual, but there weren't many of them that gave the practitioner instructions on how to do a complete ritual from beginning to end. To get rituals during that time, witches had to be initiated in a tradition or make up something by themselves.

In 1964, the first attempt to create a mass production of a Book of Shadows was done in pamphlet form, and it was trying to devalue the craft. Allegedly, the pamphlet was from Gerald Gardner himself. It was published by Mary and Charles Cardell, who were a couple but tried to pretend they were sister and brother. The Cardells allegedly received a copy of Gardner's so-called Book of Shadows from Olive Greene, who was a disgruntled associate of Gerald's. The Cardell story is odd, and it is believed that Olive was a "spy" of theirs.

This pamphlet was published privately and did not go over too well in the witchcraft community. The Cardell's attempts at publishing the Book of Shadows turned out to be a flop, and the pamphlet was soon forgotten. Another Book of Shadows that was published did much better with the public, and many have been in print for many decades. The next section looks at some of the more popular mass-produced Books of Shadows. These have all changed the world of witchcraft in their own right.

The very first book published that contained full-length rituals that resembled parts of modern witchcraft were *Mastering Witchcraft: A*

Practical Guide for Witches, Warlocks, and Covens by Paul Huson. This book was a long cry from being a Book of Shadows, and many of the spells felt more "life ceremonial magic" than witchcraft, but the book still felt familiar.

The book begins with an illustration of the Wheel of the Year before it dives straight into a bunch of spell work. He also had a bunch of invocations for deities like Diana and Cernunnos, familiar exclamations like "so mote it be," and pentacles. Most of the material in the first two-thirds of the book is interesting. It doesn't just resemble Wiccan witchcraft, but the last chapter changes all of that.

During this part of the book, Huson started to outline more than just simple spells. He gives ways to start creating a Book of shadows. He also includes a few initiation rituals. His book was the first published version of *The Charge of the Goddess*, even though it does vary from what most people are used to.

Although Huson did take a huge step forward in published witch rituals, Lady Sheba's book made the biggest, most controversial leap with her book. Her book was titled *Lady Sheba's Book of Shadows*. She claimed that she was initiated into the craft during the 1930s and that her book came from her initiation. The truth is, her book, along with her initiation, came via proxy during the 70s. She later claimed that the Goddess had pushed her to publish the book that was likely full of oath-bound rituals.

It goes without saying that Gardnerian practitioners were very upset after her book was published. The existence of the book is still a touchy subject even now. When the late 70s rolled around, Sheba had retired from the public eye. Even though her book was the first to show a ritual from start to finish, it still wasn't thought of as a complete Book of Shadows. It might have contained a lot of information about rituals, but it didn't give people a context about them. A Book of Shadows needs to be more than just a collection of rituals; it should be a source of information about the craft and give wisdom that has been passed down from generation to generation.

The next book that was published did not cause as much controversy. *The Tree: The Complete Book of Saxon Witchcraft* was published in 1974 by Raymond Buckland. It didn't break any oaths and was the first book for practitioners who worked alone. In history, Buckland was very influential in the Pagan world. He migrated from London to the United States during the early 60s. He began working with Gerald Gardner, and he and his wife were initiated into the Wiccan faith.

Even though his book did hold many similarities to the British Traditional Witchcraft, his Sabbat rituals were much different than Sheba's or Gardner's. Through his book, Buckland came up with a new Wiccan path, which he called Seax-Wica. This is still being practiced to this day. He added more to his book that Sheba's book lacked. He gave information that explained how rituals worked. For many years, his book was one of the best places for people to turn to find information about witchcraft.

Samuel Weiser, in 1978, published *A Book of Pagan Rituals*. The information inside his book was originally created by The Pagan Way group, which is still being practiced. The information was passed through periodicals and magazines during that time. Their rituals worked in two ways. Their rituals were able to be used within an Outer Court setting. Outer Court was a training circle for pre-initiates that some traditions have. And they could also be used in a public setting where they were sharing rituals.

Because most of the information was created for covens and groups, many of the rituals did not have much in the way of context, but it also gave another huge lead in distributing ritual information. It was one of the first books to have the word Pagan in the title and not the words witch or witchcraft.

Then there is Doreen Valiente, who has been called the "Mother of Modern Witchcraft". She was one of the architects and writers of the modern revival. Valiente was initiated by Gardner in 1953, and she would end up writing most of the information for the *Gardnerian Book of Shadows* and several of the other books that it influenced.

Doreen also released *Witchcraft for Tomorrow* in 1978. This was the first book on Witchcraft that was published in England that gave people full rituals for the Sabbats as well as a self-initiation ritual. This gave many people in Britain a way to get into witchcraft that was the traditional coven structure.

Then, one of the most important Witchcraft books that was published in 1979 was called *The Spiral Dance: A Rebirth of the Ancient Religion of the Great Goddess*. Starhawk did not just write a book about Gardner's Witchcraft and all of the other offshoots; rather, it gave information about a new American West Coast witchcraft. It was full of environmentalism, feminism, and all the influence of Victor and Cora Anderson. The latter were the most influential teachers of witchcraft in American history.

Starhawk did not mean for this book to be a Book of Shadows, but it pretty much was. Its pages and the information they contained felt like they had been circled tested and taken right out of a real ritual that had to have happened at his home.

As the 1980s began, Steward and Janet Farrar published *Eight Sabbats for Witches*. It was full of ceremonies and rites for people who followed the Alexandrian Witchcraft path. There was a companion book released in 1984 called *The Witches' Way: Principles, Ritual, and Beliefs of Modern Witchcraft*. Both of these books had input from Doreen, and they all thought that the book was a great way to share the Gardnerian Book of Shadows.

Some people say these books are a violation of their oaths. Valiente, though, assured them and others that they had permission to share the information.

These two books would eventually be combined to create *A Witches' Bible: The Complete Witches' Handbook*, and this would mark the

Farrars and Valiente's success at creating a Book of Shadows based on Gardner's teachings during the 50s. With the way it flows and is written, the reader knows that everything in the book has been shared exactly the way the creator of the rites wanted it to be.

Before the internet became people's main way to keep in contact with the Pagan world, there were many witches and other Pagans that stayed in contact through periodicals and magazines. Ed Fitch was a pioneer in this area, and the things he did left a lasting impression of witchcraft. He helped with the rituals of The Pagan Way, as well as putting together two "underground classics" that brought rituals to everyone.

The Outer Court Book of Shadows and the *Grimoire of the Shadows* were private publications that circulated through the 1970s, and even today, that gave coven leaders a way to share rituals without feeling like they were breaking their oaths. Besides those underground books, Fitch also created the magazine, *The Crystal Well* in 1965. In this magazine, he and Janine Renee shared Sabbat rituals.

What would become an influential Book of Shadows was first made public in 1989 and was called "Section III" in the Scott Cunningham book *Wicca: A Guide for the Solitary Practitioner*. The book was very revolutionary because it was the first widely circulated witchcraft book in the United States that used the work Wiccan in its title.

Another reason it is so powerful was that "Section III," also known as The Standing Stones Book of Shadows, held complete information about magical oils, rituals, and spells. Cunningham's book served as an entryway into the Craft, and this is still true today.

The Grimoire

The word "grimoire" is usually interchangeable with a Book of Shadows. The word is an Old French term for "grammar." It is simply a generic term for a "book of magic". These have been around for centuries. The word can be used to describe a Book of

Shadows, but not every Grimoire would be considered a Book of Shadows.

Most modern self-help books of this nature focus on the art of manifestation and are thought to have been derived from the teachings during the nineteenth century. The practices and philosophies are traced back to people like Ralph Waldo Emerson, Franz Mesmer, and Phineas Quimby, along with other acolytes. What does not get recognized as much is the influence of the "Old Magic" Grimoires had, which were sometimes called "books" or "the sorcerers".

These were probably the first books written that were concerned with manifestation that was sometimes called "elemental or low" magic. While many of their methods would come off as a bit dubious to modern people, who had become used to modern psychology and new age ideas, they are still extremely important artifacts in our culture and are fascinating historical documents behind the need for a person to realize their dreams and desires.

One of the oldest pieces of magical texts is *Sepher ha-Razin*. It is a work of Jewish magic and dates to about the third or fourth century. This book has many of the essential elements that the Grimoires that came after it had, which include shamanistic practices like attacking enemies, obtaining visions, and healing. It also contains a bit of peculiar information on invocating the Hebrew held names of God.

The Aim of Sage or *Ghayat al-Hakim* was written in Arabic and published around 1,000 and 1,150 CE. In 1250, it was translated into Spanish and then Latin. This was when it became *The Picatrix*. The information in this book came from Ancient Persian and Greek traditions. It was a manual of sorts for astral magic, as well as for instructions for pulling down the energy of the planets and stars into talismans.

During medieval times, there was an important Jewish Grimoire written that was called *The Book of Raziel the Archangel*. This was written around the thirteenth century, and became a foundation for the following Grimoires. According to the text in this book, Raziel sent secret messages to Adam and Eve after they were kicked out of Eden so that they could become divine once more.

Raziel did this without having permission to do so. This caused him to be called a rebel, and his book was taken away. In the Jewish faith, Raziel is parallel to Prometheus, the Greek God who took fire from the heavens and gave it to the humans, which incurred the wrath of Zeus.

Le Grand Albert was written in 1493 in Latin and mainly revolved around natural magic, which includes stones, herbs, how to ward off diseases, and other uses of alchemy and physiognomy. The Albert in this book's title supposedly stood for Albertus Magnus. He was a Catholic bishop who was knowledgeable in theology, science, and some occult arts, which included alchemy and astrology.

The book *On Occult Philosophy* or *De Occulta Philosophia* was a huge encyclopedia of magical lore. Heinrich Cornelius Agrippa wrote this book in 1510 and is likely one of the most influential texts ever written about low and high magic. In 1533, Trithemius, Agrippa's mentor, suggested he publish it. In 1651, it was translated into English as *Three Books of Occult Philosophy.*

In 1993, Llewellyn published another edition of the book that had been exhaustively annotated and edited by Donald Tyson. Agrippa was pretty ambiguous. Most of his works were written during his early twenties, but some pieces of information mentioned that near the end of his life, he had started to condemn his writings. Keep in mind that this was very common during the Renaissance era because they had to maneuver through the muck of ecclesiastical intolerance carefully.

In 1668, *Le Petit Albert* was written as the "little brother" of *Le Grand Albert*. It would have several reprintings throughout the next 100 years. This time, Albert did not refer to Albertus Magnus, but Albertus Parvus Licius. The book was made of several previous writings, which could have included those of Paracelsus. The

Catholic Church censored and condemned the book, which, allegedly, would become available on the French "black market" during the eighteenth and nineteenth centuries. It was very popular in rural France, and was often considered to be a "Farmer's Almanac". It contained more information about the practical uses of low magic in order to create desired changes in a person's life.

In 1801, *The Magus* was written by Francis Barrett. His text was basically a compilation of past texts, mainly *De Occulta Philosophia* and *The Heptameron*. Since it did not have much in the way of original material, it could be questioned as to why it is even making this book. There are two reasons: It was an influential piece of text at the time when these types of writing were no longer popular, and the majority of Grimoires borrowed or modified information from previous books.

This is by no means all of the ancient Grimoires that predate all of the Books of Shadows listed in the previous section. However, this does give you a good idea of what Grimoires are and how a Book of Shadows differs from these ancient texts. While you can freely call your Book of Shadows a Grimoire, remember that the first Grimoires did not have the same type of information that your Book of Shadows will have. They did not have the Sabbats of today, and as such, didn't describe rituals for them.

How to Use a Book of Shadows

When you have created your Book of Shadows, you will figure out why you like using it. For most Wiccans, they use it to help them document their spiritual journey. The biggest rule, though, that many Wiccans have is that a Book of Shadows should only include things that are related to Wiccan practice, and it should only be used by you. You should never allow anyone else to write in your Book of Shadows.

Wiccans put many things into their Books of Shadows, and the next section goes over some of them. But to get you started with your Book of Shadows, you need a journal. This could be a fancy leather-bound book with magic symbols on it, or it can just be a simple three-ring binder with some loose-leaf paper.

1. Herbology

Herbs play a huge role in witchcraft. If you use many herbs in your practice, it's a good idea that you write down whatever you know about your herbs in your Book of Shadows. Make sure you list the medicinal and magical uses of the herbs that you use the most. If it suits you, you could always add some drawings. This is where you can add tea recipes, gather information, make notes on gardening, and how to dry herbs.

2. Divination

Many witches keep tarot journals to write down their spreads and interpretations. This is a great place to collect information about various types of divination, like runes and pendulums. To get the most out of your readings, you could add in a cheat sheet with all of the associations and meanings of tarot cards, or you can write out different spreads that you would like to try.

3. Esbats and the Moon

If you like to use the moon cycles to enhance your magic, you can write down everything that you have learned about it in your Book of Shadows. You can write the moon names down with their dates and also jot down everything about their meanings or any spells that you need to do during certain phases of the moon. This could include correspondences and rituals.

4. Dreams

Your Book of Shadows is a great place to write down dreams that you have, and then try to interpret what they could mean. This might be hard for some people who either can't remember their dreams or usually don't have the time to focus on them. This is a great way to enhance your psychic powers.

5. Symbols

If you like using different symbols and sigils within your practice, then you need to write them in your book. This is a great place to put your rune, moon, zodiac, and tarot symbols so that you have a quick guide.

6. **Devotional Journal**

You could add a section to your Book of Shadows that is dedicated to your patron Deity or any other type of entity that you choose to work with.

7. Research

If you are learning new things about your craft, you could write down some notes about the things you have learned. If you are creating a new spell or ritual, you need to take some notes during your prep work. This could work as a draft of the spell, and you can put the spell into that section of your Book of Shadows once you have worked out "all of the bugs".

8. Witchy Journal

This is a more personal topic that you can journal about in your Book of Shadows. This could be about rituals or impressions that you have gotten. You could also write down plans for your magical work, draw doodles, or just write your feelings. This is a great way to help you stay in touch with your power.

9. Sacred Texts

You can write things such as incantations, poems, change, prayers, and any other type of text that means something special to you. If you have a specific deity that you believe in, you can write your prayers to them here that you use in your practice. If this isn't something you normally do, you could just write down texts that speak to you. You could use them in your practice if you would like to. You could also write your own scripts.

10. Magic Exercises and Theories

You could write down all the information concerning your magical practice in this section. This could include things like rules, correspondences, and ethics. This would be a great place to write down exercises and techniques like your energy work and psychic abilities.

11. Spells

This is the first thing that most people think of when it comes to a Book of Shadows. You can write the spells that you know, learn, and the ones you want to try within your book. If you find spells from different sources, it is always a good thing to have a single place to have them stored so you can easily find them. Also, when you start making spells, you want to write them down so that you remember them.

12. Recipes

These will be magical recipes. You can put recipes in your Book of Shadows that you use in your spells and rituals. Some great ideas are oil blends, elixirs, brews, and incense. This is very important when you consider yourself a kitchen witch. It would also be smart to keep a list of all the magical properties of your kitchen ingredients.

13. Crystals

If you are drawn to crystals, take some time to write down a list of what crystals you have as well as their healing uses. This is a very helpful and useful thing to do because there are quite a few gemstones out there that look alike. When you do this, it makes it easier to remember what you do and don't have. You could also write down any crystal-related magical practices like how to cleanse them, program, and charge your crystals, crystal grid layouts, and crystal correspondences.

14. The Wheel of the Year

You can write down all of the information that has to do with every Pagan festival during the year that you choose to celebrate. You can add in information for each Sabbat like tales, correspondences, prayers, rituals, crafts, folklore, prayers, and more.

Creating Your Book of Shadows

There are several ways you can create your Book of Shadows, but the following are some of the most frequently used:

- Notebook
- Binder
- Refillable journal
- Scrapbook
- Deck of cards

There are even some people who choose to make their Book of Shadows digital and will keep it in a word document or on Pinterest.

The next important thing that any Wiccan will do with the Book of Shadows is to make sure that it is well organized. This is a practical step because you do not want to be stuck for hours trying to find what it is you are looking for. There are two ways that you can choose to organize your Book of Shadows.

The first and simplest way is to have small journals to put your different topics in. You could have one journal with spells, another one with herbs, and then a different one for your personal journal. Scott Cunningham said you should have two main books. One would be your Book of Shadows that help your spells, and the second should be a mirror book that you use for your journal. The biggest downside to this organizational method is that there will be quite a few books that you are going to have to keep, and it would be quite hard to bring all of them to a gathering. Of course, you could keep a digital copy—that way, it is on your phone.

The second method is to combine everything. This is what many people do with their Book of Shadows. This is practical because everything will be in one place. That being said, you will want to organize the book itself. You can use tabs or whatever to separate the book into different sections so that you could easily find the section you need. It would be a great idea to create an index, key, and cover sheet so you can easily figure out where everything is located.

You could also decorate your Book of Shadows. If you are crafty, get creative and have some fun. The main thing is that your book is functional, but after that, you can go crazy and make it an extension of yourself.

Once you have started your Book of Shadows, it is a good idea to consecrate it with your energy.

The next thing is the size. If your book gets too large, you might find it hard to take with you when you go places, and you might find it hard to use. You should not look at it as a source of information; it needs to simply be a place to write down things that you find from other sources. It should be used to assimilate the things that you have read and experimented with, and then write them down in your own thoughts.

When you do write in your Book of Shadows, take the time to make it a ritual of its own. Cast a circle and light some incense, so you stay focused on what you are doing. When you are writing in your book, do not try to be perfect. If you make mistakes, that is fine. The most important thing is to listen to your intuition. If you begin to feel like you do not like your book or if there is a bunch of stuff you do not use in it, don't hesitate to throw it away and start over.

Types of Magic

There are three types of magic that you can practice: red, black, and white. Normally, Wiccans will only use white magic because they believe whatever they do will come back to them three-fold. They are not willing to risk having negative black magic come back to them three times as bad as what they did. The next section looks at each of these different types of magic.

White magic is basically magic that has a selfless or positive purpose. Most practitioners who use white magic have been called White Witches, healers, or wise women or men. White magic can be practiced through songs, prayers, blessings, incantations, healing, or charms.

In Gareth Knight's *A History of White Magic*, published in 1978, he wrote that the origins of this type of magic could be traced to the Paleolithic Era. This also includes Ancient Egypt, and there is some evidence of it being used in early Judaism and Christianity. The biggest evidence of these traditions is when people worshipped goddesses and gods of fertility and vegetation.

Toward the end of the fifteenth century, natural magic had become a huge topic amongst the high class. People who followed Marisilio Ficino believed that there were spirits and other spiritual beings. He and his followers were faced with criticism from the Catholic Church, even though the church also acknowledged these things. Ficino believed in natural magic that did not require an invocation of malevolent or malicious spirits. Johannes Trithemius would not believe in this theory of Ficino's, even though he would create incantations and spells that would help someone connect with beneficial spirits.

Magic, even white magic, can be touched within the Christian community, but within texts and early teachings, there was a dual comprehension of good and bad. This could be seen in battles between light and dark. White magicians were often called saints. They also thought that these people could control the elements bestowed on them, and they could affect many different phenomena. They would refer to these events as miracles.

Things started to change, and Christian followers believed that people who had these powers were using them for personal gain and selfish reasons. Thus, they looked at these people with very little regard because they felt they had evil intentions.

In modern times, white magic is simply magic that is done for good or to take the practitioner to a greater spiritual state of consciousness. The important thing when it comes to magic is knowing that it requires a bit of an altered conscious state and the understanding that any magic performed affects the whole world as well as the witch.

The next type of magic is *red magic*. This term is not used often, and many people haven't even heard of it. Red magic is simply the simplest form of spells. This was and is the kind of magic that simple people would use, the temple initiate, and the shaman. In early American culture, it used to be called Hoodoo.

Red magic has been referred to as sex magic. This, while it is not completely untrue, isn't an accurate or even a nice name. It makes it sound like this type of magic could be used to make poor choices. Red magic uses the life force and body within a person, just like our ancestors did. Red magic will always be the strongest when it is shared between two people, even if only one person is needed. The support, friendship, and love help to strengthen the magic of the spell. If you cannot or do not have a lover with you, then a person who is spiritually linked to the spell or a friend will do just fine.

Last, there is *black magic*. Black magic is usually referred to as the type of magic that has negative outcomes. This might include things like:

- Magic that is done to impact another person's free will.

- Magic that is meant to invoke the spirit realm for negative purposes.
- Magic that is done to bring about harm or destruction, like curses and hexes.
- Magic that is meant to be baneful, like getting rid of or restricting the actions of others.

Other traditions would refer to this type of magic as dark magic. However, it is important to remember that not all Pagan traditions split magic into simple groups like white or black. Also, the majority of magic that is cast will have a bit of an impact on the free will of people, and that is not always a bad thing. Performing magic is about making changes. Unless you only work magic on yourself, and this is completely fine, there isn't any way to perform magic without causing some influence on someone or something else.

When you are doing spiritual work, there is a chance that you might conjure up something that you did not want to. If you are putting your energy into working with spirits and you don't put as much into protective measures, then that is just asking for trouble.

Just like with so many things in life, what one person sees as negative intent is simply another person's view of getting things done. Do not be surprised if you find people inside the Wiccan community that frown upon anybody who does magic that could be considered as "black". They will sometimes refer to people who do some "negative" magic as taking the "left-hand path." The fact of the matter is: It all depends on what you feel on the inside. A person may warn you against a certain coven or Wiccan path because they do things that the person does not believe in, but that doesn't mean it would not work for you.

More often than not, you are going to hear black magic used by non-Pagans to describe all types of magic without them being willing to learn anything about it. The bottom line when it comes to performing any magic is that you have to go with your gut and intuition. If you feel safe doing it, and you do not think it is really going to do any harm, then do it. As long as you are okay with whatever repercussions could come back, then it is your path to take.

Wicca

If you were to ask ten people what Wicca is, you would probably get ten different responses; likewise, if you asked those same ten people when Wicca originated. Many people assume things about Wicca based on things they have seen on television, social media, and what they have heard in Bible class. Some things are tinged on the truth, while others are outright ignorant.

This is not about bashing religion though. There isn't one right path, and people have the right to follow whatever belief system they choose. However, it is important to know the real story of how the religion began, what it is based on, and what it truly means to be Wiccan. This chapter provides you with such information.

Do not be surprised if you learn things that don't coincide with what you have previously heard and read. As mentioned, there is a lot of different information out there from millions of different sources and people. Wicca is further for men just as much as it is for women—this seems to be a misconception that must be dispelled now. Many people also believe that Wicca is only for empowered women, but it is not; Wicca welcomes everyone from all walks of life. There are not any prerequisites to being Wiccan.

What is Wicca?

You are getting ready to learn about how Wicca draws upon the Old Traditions of witchcraft. This is true, but first, it needs to be clarified that Wicca and witchcraft, while very similar, are not the same thing. A person does not have to be a Wiccan to be a witch, much like a person doesn't have to be a Baptist to be a Christian. Wicca is a religion, but witchcraft is not. It may be safer to say that Wicca is very much a modern religion that has roots based on ancient traditions.

Contrary to some beliefs or lies that have circulated, Wicca is a very peaceful and harmonious life path that works by promoting a connection with the divine.

Wicca is seeing love in nature. It is enjoying the sunrise and sunset. It is seeing the dew on the flowers in the morning and the bright colors of seasons. The gentle movement of one's hair as the wind blows it and the warmth of the Sun on one's skin. It is the tweet of birds and the hello of all wild creatures. It is living with Mother Earth and being humbled by Her power. When working with the divine, make sure your arrogance and technology are not affecting you.

When a person is a witch, they are protecting, giving, seeking, healing, and teaching all things. If this is the path that you feel led to follow, then travel on it with honor and integrity.

Wicca's belief system originated in pre-Christian Wales, Scotland, and Ireland. While much of the information about the way our ancestors believed, lived, and worshipped has been lost due to the medieval church's efforts to wipe out their existence, we are trying to reconstruct all of those beliefs the best we can with what information is available.

Based on archaeological discoveries, many of the parts of the belief system date to the Paleolithic Era, where people would worship the Fertility Goddess and the Hunter God. Cave paintings from around 30,000 years ago were discovered to depict a man with the head of a stag, and a pregnant woman standing within a circle of eleven people. This could indicate that witchcraft is the oldest belief system. It is easy to see that many Wiccan traditions predate Christianity by about 28,000 years.

Witchcraft has often been referred to as "The Craft of the Wise," in ancient history because the followers were more connected to nature, understood medicines and herbs, gave council, and played very important parts in the community and village as leaders and healers. They understood that man was not superior to nature, its creatures, and the Earth, but were a single aspect of many different parts, both of the seen and unseen aspects that created a larger whole.

These wise people understood that everything that was used or taken from the earth needs to be replenished to keep the delicate balance. In modern times, this notion has been forgotten. This is likely the main reason why we are facing an ecological disaster because of people's need for power.

Over the last several hundred years, the views of a witch have been created to appear unrighteous, evil, and hedonistic, and there are a couple of places where these misconceptions started.

The best place to begin is between the fifteenth and eighteenth centuries with the medieval church. They came up with a bunch of stories about witchcraft to try and get people to convert to their religion. By turning the witch into an evil creature and switching the old religion's deities into demons and devils, their missionaries would attach fear to this belief system, which helped during their conversions process.

The second place where misconceptions started was as medical science began to state its place in the world; the men who studied these things did not understand how the female boy worked, especially when it came to menstruation. The unknown information in this area worked perfectly into the agenda of the early church, which helped witch hunters find their footing. The medical professionals benefited a lot from all of this since it removed power from the women healers and made people trust the male physicians more, giving them more power and respect.

Unfortunately, all of these beliefs have continued through the years, and many are still prevalent today. This is the reason why many use the name Wicca instead of witchcraft to keep from being persecuted and harassed.

Now to a shift of focus. What is Wicca? In Wicca, followers have two deities, the Goddess and the God. They make up the female and male aspects of the life force that creates everything, and this also includes life and death. The deities are worshipped at different times during the year. Festivals that worship the God are called sabbats. These correspond with the position of the Earth to the Sun and include the equinoxes, solstices, and the cross-quarter days between these points. The Goddess is worshipped during every Full Moon, which is known as the Esbats.

When you put all of these celebrations together, they make up the Wheel of the Year. With this type of worldview, death is viewed as an important part of ongoing life, as the old has to leave to make way for the new. The shadow of life, which is the "dark of the Moon" right before it becomes new, is just as important as life. Some types of Wicca have the tradition of "dark half" and "light half" of the year, which are marked by the summer and winter solstices.

Wicca is very unique. First, unlike the more common monotheistic, organized religions, Wicca does not have a designated center of worship. Instead, it consists of a decentralized community of individuals and groups who can worship publicly, in their homes, or in nature. All of which can either be done with others or alone.

Second, Wiccans do not have an official "holy book" or a specific ideology that every practitioner has to adhere to. While there are many beliefs that most Wiccans have in common, there isn't a single way of understanding things that are viewed as being "correct" more so than others. For example, some have a pantheistic view, which means they believe the same source of the divine is present in every area of nature, while others view things in a more polytheistic way, using one or more deities for past religions in their practice.

This fluidity of the belief system is very much welcomed by those who discover the religion. This is because it allows and encourages people to find their own truth as they travel their spiritual path. There is also an infinite number of paths that can be placed under the term Wicca.

Many people who want to know "what is Wicca?" are interested in magic. The reason for this is that most, but not all, Wiccans will use their connection with divine energies to shape their lives, as well as to help others. This is why it's known as magic. Magic is much older than Wicca and not exclusive to Wicca, but there are many common characteristics of this practice among the followers of Wicca.

First, magic is often used during rituals people hold during the Esbats and Sabbats, and many Wiccans perform spell work during the New Moon. Wiccan magic typically uses different tools and ingredients like herbs, crystals, candles, and spoken affirmations and chants. They might even call upon certain deities for assistance in manifesting what they want.

The most important part of Wiccan magic is The Wiccan Rede, which states "harm to none." This basically means that magic must be for positive purposes. It should not cause harm to other people, be it deliberate or not. Wiccans follow this very seriously, as it helps to keep a harmonious balance with everything that exists.

While you can still find traditional covens that follow the lineage of the creation of Wicca, much of what is practiced bears little resemblance to what Wicca started out as in the 1940s and 50s. The majority of Wiccans are solitary witches who haven't been initiated into a certain tradition but borrow from different places to make their own eclectic practice.

This phenomenon, along with the increase in popularity of this faith, has created a rich and diverse religion that evolves every day. For people who are new to this, the differing and conflicting information about Wicca can seem daunting. However, for the people who are drawn to creating their own life paths, the diversity within Wicca is very rewarding.

Story of Wicca

Many people refer to Wicca as "The Old Religion." Many even say that it is a tradition that families have passed down through the years, and was hidden during the Christians purge of Pagans until they knew that it could make a safe emergence. This sense of it being such ancient history is the main reason why people are attracted to Wicca. After all, with the industrialized, noisy world around us, many people need something wiser and older than themselves? But what are the actual origins of Wicca?

If speaking literally, Wicca is by no means ancient, or all that old. In fact, it was only established in the mid-twentieth century, but its influences are very much old. You can view the history of Wicca in two ways: The story of how it was founded in England during the 1940s and 50s, and as a bigger part of a mythical story of a quest to connect and understand all of the mysteries of the Universe. While you can only verify one of these, both are just as important to understanding the story of Wicca.

The creation of the religion that ended up becoming Wicca was established by Gerald Gardner, who was an author, occultist, and civil servant. Gardner was born in 1884. He was a traveler and was interested in things like archaeology, folklore, spiritualism, and anthropology. He became part of several societies and clubs that focused on his interests, which included him joining a Rosicrucian

Order in 1939. Within this group, he met some people who had created a secretive group, and who eventually let Gardner know that they were a coven of witches. In September of the same year, he was initiated into their coven.

During the 1920s, a theory had started to travel in the anthropological circles about a nature-based religion that Christianity had just about stamped out, but there were still groups of practitioners throughout Western Europe. Margaret Murray, the creator of this theory, called it a "Witch-cult," and said that those who still practiced it were a part of thirteen-member covens. After meeting the New Forest group, Gardner believed that they ought to be a part of this pre-Christian religion, and wanted to make sure that this witch-cult survived through the twentieth century.

Then in the 1940s, Gardner continued to study different spiritual and religious ideas and traditions but was impacted strongly by what he learned with the New Forest coven. Eventually, he would come up with his own named Bricket Wood, and started to create a new iteration of the witch-cult. All of his inspiration came from various sources, which also included the New Forest coven, parts of the Freemasons, ceremonial magic, and many other figures in the occult world. He drew inspiration from people like Cecil Williamson and Aleister Crowley. One of the biggest additions that Gardner created ended up becoming one of the most important elements of Wicca: worshipping both the Goddess and God, who were completely equal. This was a very unique view, considering the age he lived in was very male-dominated.

Gardner never gave his religion the name of Wicca. He would sometimes call his coven members "the Wicca." They would call people who performed divination and sorcerers that in Old English. Witchcraft was what their tradition was often called, sometimes as "the Craft," or "the Old Religion." It was at least another decade before it became known as Wicca as it started to spread throughout Australia and the United States.

At this point, there were different versions of Gardner's creation that created other occultists and followers, some that didn't look very much like the original coven. The United Kingdom practitioners that continued to follow what Gardner had laid out call themselves the British Traditional Witchcraft. These practitioners did not view Wicca as the same practice they followed, tending to simply call it an American creation. However, other places in the world referred to the original Wicca as Gardnerian Wicca.

While Gardner did give modern witchcraft a boost, he did not do all of this alone; in fact, many important people helped create Wicca. There were many colleagues and friends of Gardner who took part in the collaboration, which included Doreen Valiente, Patricia Crowther, and Lois Bourne. Then there were other occultists of the mid-twentieth century, like Raymond Buckland and Robert Cochrane. Indeed, the complete history of Wicca and the development of it could fit inside many books, and still, the whole story probably would not be told.

Much inspiration for these modern occultists came from the British occult revival during the late nineteenth century, and many things date back to the thirteenth century. Those people drew their inspiration from ancient civilizations.

Wiccan Belief System

There are several different offshoots of the Wiccan religion. These include:

- Celtic
- Family Tradition
- Eclectic
- Gardnerarian
- Circle Craft
- Alexandrian

- Faerie
- Shamanic
- Dianic
- British Traditionalist

Within the majority of Wiccan traditions, along with most other Pagan traditions, there are several types of groups and individual practitioners. Groups will differ in ritual practices, symbology orientation, purpose, structure, size, and several other ways. Some require an initiation, while others do not. The initiation will vary depending on the traditions and can include initiations by groups, and self-initiations.

While there are quite a few differences, there are also some philosophies and spiritual practices that Wiccans and other Pagans have in common. The biggest similarity is that they both love and respect Nature and seek to reach harmony with the ecosphere. The next section looks at some of the belief systems within the Wiccan faith.

The Goddess and Triple Goddess

Many Wiccan traditions that celebrate a three-fold goddess known as the Triple Goddess. The aspects are the Maiden, Mother, and Crone and are connected to the Moon's travels. These are also the same aspects of the three phases of the woman's life when it comes to physical reproduction.

While women proceed linearly through phases of life, every part of the Triple Goddess has qualities within everything, and they are connected with different aspects of life. Indeed, the different phases of the Goddess can show the complexity of the human mind, and the life and death that everyone will experience.

The creation of this triple deity can be linked to many old civilizations like Brighid, who was a Celtic goddess and ruled over the main skills: smithcraft, healing, and poetry. There is also Hera.

She played three roles in Ancient Greece: Girl, Woman, and Widow. These are probably a small part of the inspiration for the creation of an important Wiccan text: *The White Goddess: A Historical Grammar of Poetic Myth* by Robert Graves.

The British scholar and poet Graves wrote during the same era as Gerald Gardner started to practice his form of witchcraft, which became Wicca. His book stated that cultures in the Ancient Middle East and pre-Christian Europe worshipped a White goddess known as the Birth, Love, and Death. In each region, she was given a different name. Other, earlier writers also talked about a Triple Goddess, which included Sigmund Freud and Aleister Crowley.

Gardner did not have a Triple Goddess that he worshipped in his tradition, but plenty of others have been drawn to one, which included Robert Cochrane, who tends to be credited for bringing the Triple Goddess into modern witchcraft. The 1970s is when the Triple Goddess of today became rooted in several Wiccan paths.

However, instead of being one identity that takes on different forms, the Triple Goddess tends to have three different deities representing her. These are typically borrowed from different cultures. Some worship the Maiden as Diana, the Mother as Isis, and the Crone as Kali.

Each of the Triple Goddess' aspects is associated with a specific season or phenomena, and human aspects of Earth. People can use these to call on the most appropriate goddess for their rituals or spells.

The Triple Goddess is symbolized in a Full Moon with the waning and waxing crescents on either side.

The Maiden part of the Triple Goddess is connected to the crescent-to-waxing phase of the Moon. This is the youthful part of life. During this time, there is growth, as you can see in the Moon as it becomes fuller. As for Nature, the Maiden is the spring, sunrise, and dawn.

The Maiden is representative of new and potential life and beauty. In humans, she is independence, intelligence, self-confidence, youth, and innocence. She is associated with activities such as creativity, exploration, self-expression, and discovery. The Goddesses that can be used to worship the Maiden are Persephone, Freya, Artemis, and Rhiannon, but there are also many others.

As the Moon becomes full, the Maiden turns to the Mother, having given birth to the abundance of the Earth. She is the summer, midday, and the lush time of the year. She is also the fullness of life, adulthood, responsibility, and nurturing in humans.

Being the giver of life that she is, she is often used for manifestation. Many Wiccans view the Mother as being the most powerful aspect of the Goddess. Some goddesses that can be used to represent the Mother are Ceres, Badb, Selene, Danu, and Demeter.

Then, as the Moon begins to wane, and the darkness begins to grow in the sky, the Crone comes into power. In early iterations of the Triple Goddess, she was often called the hag. She is the post-childbearing years, and her seasons are winter and autumn, night and sunset, and the end of the growing season. The Crone is the wise one and is in control of guidance, prophecy, visions, transformations, past lives, death and rebirth, endings, and aging.

While this aspect has been feared for a long time, she is the one who makes sure we always remember that death is a completely normal aspect of the cycle of life, just like the sky becomes dark before the Moon begins to grow. Some of the goddesses that can represent the Crone are Cailleach Bear, Morrigan, Baba Yaga, and Hecate.

The Goddess is very much a complex and diverse expression of divine femininity. For the followers who choose to worship the Goddess, she will provide them with constant opportunities to help them grow and learn through her three aspects. Whether you decide to see every part of the Goddess, or you simply honor the Maiden, Mother, and Crone, you have the power to consciously align your worship with the Moon phases to reach a deeper and rewarding spiritual connection.

Horned and Sun Gods

This is the masculine part of life and is typically connected to the Sun and the horned animals. When he is the God of the Hunt, he will sometimes be a man wearing a headdress of antlers or horns, or he will be a man with the head of a goat or stag. This role of his is two-fold, as he helps the humans in finding sustenance through wild game, but he also helps to protect the animals, making sure that there is a constant balance of life.

During the early forms of Wicca, the Horned God was associated with fertility, and this can still be found today in some traditions. Besides the Celtic god Cernunnos, the Horned God can also be represented by Herne, Pan, Bran, and many more. There is another representation known as the Green Man, who is a mysterious, ancient archetype that people have had all over the world. He is often depicted as a human face surrounded by or made up of vines, leaves, and other foliage.

The other main association of God is with the Sun, whose light is seen to be a part of the male energy and is needed for growth. Many ancient cultures worshipped an Earth Mother and Sky Father in some form or another, which Wicca emulates to an extent. With the Wiccan Wheel of the Year, it lives with the relationship of the Earth Goddess and the Sun God, with the God dying off in the autumn and being reborn in the spring, which echoes the growth of plants. Some common Sun Gods are Lugh, Ra, and Apollo.

The Spiral of Rebirth

When it comes to rebirth, it can be a controversial topic. This idea of rebirth is a big lesson in Wicca. As discussed, every year, there is a birth, growth, and death. This is the same truth for human life, as well. All of this continues on and on through the spiral of rebirth.

Like with many other religions, people are reincarnated in order to perfect the soul. A single lifetime is not enough to reach this goal. This is why the soul is reborn several times.

The soul is ageless, non-physical, sexless, and contains parts of the divine Goddess and God. Every time the soul manifests in the real world, it is different. No two bodies are the same, or lives for that matter. The soul would end up stagnating if it came back into the same life after a time. The economic class, birthplace, race, sex, and every other part that makes up a person is determined by what the soul did during past lives and what lessons it needs to learn.

Afterlife

A common question people have about Wicca, and the spiral of rebirth is, "What is the afterlife?" Many religions try to explain what it will be like after our life on Earth is over. Everybody has different views on this subject.

Wicca does not try to answer to this subject. There is no scripture, not accepted doctrines or revelations about what is in the afterlife, or if there even is one. There are very different views within Wicca itself when it comes to the subject, but there is no "official" stance. This means that any conclusions that have been reached are all individual beliefs. There isn't an authority that tells you what you should believe about what happens after death.

The main belief in Wicca, as mentioned, is reincarnation. The next section looks at some lesser-known afterlife beliefs first.

Summerland is one. Some people mistakenly believe that this is the Wiccan word for "heaven", but that is not really accurate from a Judeo-Christian perspective.

Some Wiccans believe that there is life after death and another plane of existence. This would be the spirit world that is located behind the veil, where the spirits travel to rest and reunite. Summerland is simply a name for this world, but nobody actually knows what it is like.

Some believe that you are in control of what your afterlife will be and become. There is a bit of a caveat, though, as since your thoughts can create whatever you want in your afterlife, if you have a negative, pessimistic soul, you could easily end up creating your own personal "hell" of an afterlife.

Then some Wiccans believe that the soul is simply immortal and free from the body when we die. There is not a certain place they travel to, and reincarnation is simply one option. Once a person is unshackled from their physical body, the spirit can roam the expanses of space and time.

It is kind of like being in a permanent state of astral travel. One minute you can choose to travel to watch the pyramids being built, and the next, you could be on Pluto far into the future when it is being colonized. You can watch whatever you want to, or you can sleep, and never wake up unless you choose to come back.

Another afterlife idea overlaps the other two. This is that some spirits can become "trapped". This could be due to unfinished business, living through trauma, not realizing they are dead, or their negativity traps them. Either way, some souls cannot move on to the afterlife, or roam through the Universe, or be reincarnated until they can be released from Earth.

These are the entities and ghosts that people believe haunt certain places. Not all Wiccan believe that there are ghosts or an afterlife—some think that death is just the end. These are the Wiccans that watch the leaves fall off the trees in the fall, but say the ones that return in the spring are not the same. The way they see it is when we fall, the life energy is taken in by the Universe, and we simply move on. The body becomes food for the Earth. They merely think life after death is wishful thinking or fear of mortality.

Overall, Wicca is one religion that is not all that concerned about the afterlife. We may be curious and have our thoughts, but Wicca is mainly about the way that we live our lives, not what happens once we die.

Reincarnation

As mentioned, many Wiccan and Pagans believe in reincarnation. This means that they also believe in past lives. The unfortunate thing is that they do not know what past lives they have lived, and it can take quite a bit of work to learn this information.

The things that you do in your current life, or the things you did in your past life, follow you, and they will determine what you will face in your next life. A goal should be to better ourselves, and reincarnation gives us that chance. Basically, you should take whatever you are given in this life and do the best that you can.

There are things you can do to try and find out information concerning your past lives. You can use past-life regression, trance work, and use psychics. You have to be careful with this, though, because some people out there are frauds and will just try to trick you out of your money.

Taking the time to learn from your past lives can help you to figure out reasons for problems you are dealing with now, especially if you feel like you are stuck or making the same mistakes. Hopefully, learning more about your past life will help you to improve this current life.

Whether you want to learn more about your past lives, or you are more interested in focusing on your current one, the knowledge that the things you do matter should inspire you to make the most out of your life lessons.

Paganism

Paganism has been defined as anybody involved in any religious ceremony, practice, or act that is not Christian. Muslims and Jews also use the term to refer to anyone outside their religion. Others will define it as a religion other than Judaism, Buddhism, Christianity, and Hinduism; others still will define it as not having a religion.

Paganism refers to the ancient religions of Rome and Greece and the surrounding areas. It has origins in the Stone Age. The word Pagan comes from the Latin word *paganus* that means "a country dweller". Pagans normally believe in many gods. They only choose one to worship that represents the Supreme Godhead.

As Christianity came into the present age, Pagans began to mean anybody that was not a Christian. Paganism became a non-Christian religion or belief. If a religion did not fit into the Judeo-Christian-Islamic or Eastern mold, then the person practicing that religion was considered a Pagan.

History

Paganism records refer to how worshipping many deities, goddesses, and gods was viewed by many as important to their worship. They believed that everything has a spirit and was polytheistic. This gave a person the ability to have a goddess or god of the sea, forest, and any aspect of nature.

When civilizations started to change, the gods grew and changed. People started to acquire gods of their occupations. They still had their old gods, but they changed them according to their lives. Gods have always played important roles in all aspects of society. They influence everything from customs, laws, to the general working of a community. Reincarnation was readily believed by the Pagans, but they do not believe in a hell or heaven.

Nowadays, Paganism celebrates nature, all living things, the Earth, and so much more. Most modern Pagans have more than one god. Others might be atheists.

Religions and Systems

Most American Pagans practice different forms of this tradition, but the most popular are Norse, Ancient Egyptian, Native American, Greco-Roman, and Celtic.

Here is a list of others:

- **Discordianism:** This started as a Buddhist practice. The main idea was "existence is orderly chaos." Pain and pleasure, order and chaos, enlightenment and confusion, and meditative procedures are revealed as inseparable parts of a total vision.

- **Druidism:** Ancient Druids were priestesses and a part of the Ancient Celts.

- **Egyptian:** This is still popular today and involves magical and complex spiritual systems that center on rebirth and death. It was developed in Ancient Egypt when priests and priestesses were known for the skills in magic and knowledge.

- **Shamanism:** This has been practiced by Native Americans. Drumming is a traditional technique. The shaman will travel to the spirit realm to get information about the needs of the community, such as spiritual growth or healing.

- **Kabbalah:** This is a Jewish magical and mystical system that was developed during the Middle Ages.

Compared to Christianity

It is hard to compare Paganism to Christianity because the term Pagan is used to identify many different beliefs and sects.

Here are the major differences:

- Christianity will teach that Jesus was God's Son, and he came to Earth as a baby born to a virgin. He grew up, died on a cross for the sins of the entire world, and then came back to life before he ascended into heaven. Some Pagans think that Jesus is one of the gods, but don't put as much significance on Him as Christians do.

- Christianity will teach that the Bible is God's word and His message to humans. It is to be taken as it is. It is inerrant and infallible. Paganism doesn't have just one main text or a set of beliefs to follow.

- Christianity believes in only one god, where Pagans believe in many or none at all.

The Sabbats

The Wiccan belief system has what is known as the Wheel of the Year. In the Wheel, there are eight holidays known as the Sabbats. These give the practitioners a chance to gather and celebrate. The Sabbats are made up of the four "solar holidays", the equinoxes and solstices that show the journey the Earth is taking around the sun, and then the four "Earth festivals", which happen in February, May, August, and October. They mark the "cross-quarter days" that mark the midpoint between the solar points.

Wiccans do not just observe the Sabbats; many contemporary Pagans observe the Sabbats, too. Just like Wiccan information, the way the Sabbats are celebrated varies, but there is usually some ritual that focuses on a type of element of the Goddess and God relationship and season. The ritual is usually followed by a feast. These could be elaborate or simple. The way the rituals look and feel, along with the decorations and food, all depend on the Sabbat.

- **Yule/Winter Solstice**

This Sabbat occurs between December 20 and 23. Yule is usually the beginning of the Wiccan year. It is usually celebrated on December 21, but the exact timing changes each year due to the misalignment between the Earth's rotation and the Gregorian calendar. Yule is the same thing as Winter Solstice.

Yule is a fire festival and is meant to celebrate the coming light. From this point on, the days begin to get longer until it reaches the Summer Solstice. During Yule, the God gets reborn after he died during Samhain. This is a celebration of the renewed life, but when compared to other Sabbats, it is subdued and quiet since people gather in their warm homes. Wiccans usually decorate their altars with inter flora and evergreens.

Candles are important for the Sabbat, but most traditions will use red, white, green, and gold. If you have a fireplace, burn a Yule log. Many traditions are thought to be a part of Christmas that include decorated trees, caroling, wreaths, and the Yule log. These are all based on pre-Christian Pagan traditions.

- **Imbolc**

This Sabbat occurs on February 2. This Sabbat is the coming of the end of winter and the beginning of the growth in the Northern Hemisphere. This Sabbat gives thanks for the daylight as the God is growing stronger. This is a holiday for renewal and beginnings; Imbolc is usually when most initiations are done. It is a good time for cleansings after being shut inside for a few months. Some witches will put their tools out in the sun to cleanse and charge them.

Traditional colors for this holiday are orange, red, yellow, and white. Altar decorations are besoms, images of young animals, spring flowers, and figurines. Imbolc is an Irish word that is connected to the birthing of the first lambs and is translated to “ewe’s milk”.

- **Ostara**

This Sabbat occurs between March 19 and 23. This is the second spring festival. This is the time to celebrate the balance between extremes that are found in some seasons. While some regions might still be chilly, this is the official start of spring. This is the Vernal or Spring Equinox. The earth is getting warmer and more fertile. The promise of greener, warmer, and bountiful times is becoming more apparent as the buds and blossoms begin to emerge. Bees are starting to pollinate, and grass wakes out of its slumber. This is a good time to plant seeds for what you want to manifest in the next few months.

Christians usually use this time to celebrate Easter. Easter is another holiday that has its roots in Ancient Pagan customs like painting eggs, and rabbits have always been used as a fertility symbol.

- **Beltane**

This Sabbat occurs between April 30 to May 1. This is the transition between spring and summer. This is a time full of fertility, lust, and passion. This marks the return of vitality to the Sun and Earth. Blooms on plants are growing, young animals are getting more mature, and the Sun shines more.

Love and commitment are common themes of this Sabbat, along with creativity and abundance. The Wiccan wedding ceremony of handfasting is usually held at Beltane.

A common custom of this holiday is dancing around the Maypole. This pole represents the male virility. Typically, people will gather up green branches and flowers to decorate the Maypole, or they will use brightly-colored ribbons.

- **Litha**

This Sabbat occurs between June 20 and 22. This celebrates the Summer Solstice. This is the longest day of the year and marks the pinnacle of the Sun's power and the power for growth. From now on, the Sun will start to set earlier each night.

Ancient Pagans celebrated this with bonfires and torchlight processions to strengthen the Sun. This is a good time to gather wild herbs for magic and medicine since most of it is fully grown by midsummer. Another name for Litha is Midsummer, which is an older name that emphasizes the actual course of the warm months. People used to think that May 1 was the first day of summer, and this would place June 21 as the midpoint of the summer season. Litha can be traced to an old Anglo-Saxon word, *June*. It started being used for this Sabbat in the second half of the twentieth century.

- **Lammas**

This Sabbat occurs either on August 1 or 2. This is the halfway point between the Summer Solstices and the Autumn Equinox. This marks the beginning of the harvest season. This is usually the hottest part of the year and also when you can begin noticing the first bits of autumn. The days are getting shorter, trees begin releasing fruit, and the first grains can be harvested. This is the time to give thanks for the abundance.

The rituals for Lammas are normally related to harvest, gratitude, and setting intentions over the year. Making bread is a great way to mark this holiday. Some people refer to this Sabbat as Lughnasa, after the Celtic festival. Lughnasa is meant to honor the god Lugh, who is also a Sun god. Some Pagans would celebrate this holiday with sports as well as harvest festivities.

- **Mabon**

This Sabbat occurs between September 21 and 24. This is the second harvest festival like Ostara. Its days and nights are equal. The temperatures might still be warm, but summer has come to an end. The leaves will be changing colors, and the evening air will have a chill to it. Mabon is full of gratitude for the God and Goddess because it is at the height of the harvest season.

This holiday is sometimes called the Wine Harvest or Second Harvest. Mabon only started being used for this Sabbat in the later twentieth century. Magon was a Welsh figure who is connected to the divine "mother and son", which echoes the nature of the Goddess and God relationship.

- **Samhain**

This Sabbat occurs between October 31 and November 1. This is the last harvest of the year. This marks the end of the growing season and makes the beginning of winter. People have to now prepare for winter. People will dry their herbs and store them over the winter, vegetables and fruits are preserved and canned, and the root vegetables are harvested and stored to help people get through the cold months. Samhain comes from an Old Irish word, and many believe it means "Summer's end".

Thanks to Halloween, Samhain is the most visible Sabbat. Many Halloween traditions have grown from customs from Pagan times. Dating back to Ancient Greece, people have left offerings of food to their ancestors, which can be seen in the modern tradition of trick-or-treating. They would also hollow out root vegetables and a light candle in them to help guide their spirit, which is where jack-o-lanterns come from.

White Magic Spells

This first spell chapter will look at lots of white magic spells. White magic tends to be the most common magic practiced. It is magic that is used for good or positive things. Most of the time, white magic spells cannot be used to influence another person, but instead, it helps to align yourself with what it is that you want in life. This will be divided into different categories: crystal, color, herbal, candle, and bath magic.

Bath Magic

All of these spells have a common theme, besides being white magic—they all take place in a bathtub.

Aura Cleansing Bath

It is important to clean your aura from time to time, and this is a good spell to do before a big ritual so that you are ready. You should not do this bath at six a.m., noon, five p.m., or midnight. Neither should you do this during the 30 minutes before and after.

Before taking your bath, clean the tub carefully and then take a shower and clean yourself.

Make sure that you have at least an hour where you won't be disturbed. You can also light some incense and candles or play a bit of relaxing music. Do whatever relaxes you.

Fill your bathtub up with warm water, making sure it is not too hot. You can fill it as full as you would like.

Add a few good handfuls of salt into your bathwater. This could be sea salt or Himalayan salt. Epsom salt works well, too. You should not use regular table salt because there are anti-caking agents in it.

If you want, you can add some pure essential oils into your tube. Lavender is a good option because it can help you relax.

Get into the tub and soak for twenty to 30 minutes. As you do this, set the intention to release your negativity. You can ask to be the release of any energy that is not helping you—and ask to have your vibrations raised.

Once you are done, if you can, let yourself air dry. You can towel-dry your hair and wrap yourself in a robe, but do not dry your body off with a towel. Also, it is best to go 24 hours without another shower or bath.

Purification and Protection Bath

This is a great bath if you have been around people who have left you feeling out of control or negative.

Begin by steeping a teaspoon of basil in a cup of boil water. Fill your tub with warm water, as full as you want it to be. Strain the basil out of the cup of water and then pour the cup of basil water into your bathwater. Swirl it around so that it infuses the tub.

Get into the bath and relax. Allow the basil to bathe you in its protective and cleansing energy. Relax here for as long as you would like. This will remove any energy that has left you feeling negative or unclean and leave you feeling protected.

Once you are done, dry off and try to relax for the rest of the day. This is best if you can do this right before bed so that you can go straight to bed after your bath.

Rejuvenating Bath

This bath can help to relieve sinus problems and cold symptoms. It can also ease your muscular pain and increase your metabolism.

You will need:

- ½ cup of rose petals, mint leaves, elderflowers, and yarrow flowers

Place all of these herbs into the middle of a cheesecloth and tie it closed. Fill your tub with warm water and place your cheesecloth sack into the water. Let the bath herbs steep in your bathwater.

Get into the bath and relax in the water, feeling the healing and rejuvenating energy of the herbs. You can also use the cheesecloth sack to wash with. This will exfoliate your body while also healing your body.

You can stay here as long as you want.

Bath for Peace

This bath can ease a worrisome mind, or it can simply be used to help you relax before heading off to bed.

Begin by filling your tub up with warm water. Add a tablespoon of milk to a bowl of water as you say, "Water ripples on the breeze."

Add in some rose petals, which can be dried or fresh, into the bowl. Then say, "Thistledown flies through the air."

Mix everything in the bowl with your index finger on your right hand. Then say, "Silent as the mighty seas."

Carefully pour the bowl into the bath you have filled as you say, "Peaceful here without a care." Get into the bath and rest for as long as you would like. Allow the water to take away all of your negative worries and thoughts. Make sure you let your body take in as much healing peace as it can from the bath.

Be Seen More Attractively

This bath will help you appear more attractive to that special someone. Begin by filling your tub with water and then sprinkle some fresh rose petals into the water. Light a bit of vanilla incense or vanilla-scented candles.

Get into the water and relax. Allow yourself to meditate on the type of image that you would like to project outwards. Really think about how you would like other people to see you. Say, "Earth, Air, Fire, and Water, let the Goddess' beauty shine through me."

Relax here for as long as you would like.

Lover's Bath

This bath is meant to help strengthen your relationship with your significant other. You can either take a bath by yourself, or you can kick up the power of the spell by having your significant other take a bath with you.

You will need:

- A drop of sandalwood oil
- A drop of bergamot oil
- Two drops of clary sage
- Four drops of ylang

Draw a bath and then add in the essential oils. Swish everything around, so the oils are distributed throughout the bath. Light some candles and play some soft music. Get into the bath and allow yourself to relax.

If you are taking the bath alone, get out when you feel ready to. If you and your partner are bathing together, let the bath take you where it will.

Bath to Attract Love

This bath will help you to draw love into your life. It is not used to attract a specific person.

You will need:

- A pink candle
- A pinch of vervain
- ¼ teaspoon of rosemary
- One tablespoon of yarrow
- ¼ teaspoon of orris root powder

Add all of the herbs into a piece of cheesecloth and tie it closed. Fill your bath and drop the cheesecloth into the water to let it start diffusing. Once the bath is filled, light the candle and get in.

Sit in the bathwater and relax. Start to think about the type of relationship you would like to attract into your life. Picture the type of person you would like to spend your life with. Once you feel you have soaked long enough, get out of the bath, making sure that you do not use soap or rinse yourself. You want to keep the beauty of the bath on your skin.

Go to the candle and thank the Goddess and God for their help and then blow out the candle.

Candle Magic

Candle magic is a very popular type of magic, and it is probably one of the easiest, next to bath magic.

Lucky Candle Spell

Before jumping into this spell, many candle spells require you to anoint the candle with certain oils. Some spells will tell you exactly how to anoint; others won't. In general, if a spell does not tell you how, if the spell is meant to draw something into your life, you will run your finger from the top of the candle down to the bottom towards you. If the spell is getting rid of something, then you would run your finger from the bottom of the candle up to the top, away from you.

You will need:

- An orange candle
- Cinnamon oil

This spell needs to be done at midnight. Once you have cast your circle and centered yourself, begin by anointing your orange candle with the oil. You should pull your finger down the candle towards you because you are bringing in luck.

Set the candle in its holder, light it, and say: "Brimstone, moon, and witch's fire, candlelight's bright spell. Good luck I shall acquire. Work thy magic well, midnight twelve, the witching hour, bring the luck I seek. By wax and wick now work thy power as these words I speak. Harming none, this spell is done. By the law of three, so mote it be."

You can sit in meditation for a while if you want, but you should let the candle burn out. You do not want to blow out the candle if at all possible. Remember: Never leave a burning candle unattended.

Intention Candle

You will need:

- A candleholder
- Matches
- A safety pin or toothpick
- A white votive candle

Start by taking the safety pin or toothpick and carving your wish or intention into the candle. This could be anything from love or romance to health and protection—whatever you want it to be as long as it is positive and good.

Hold the candle between your hands and speak your intention out loud over and over again as you start to picture a white light flowing into and around your candle.

Set the candle in a safe place, like a holder, and then light it. Allow the candle to burn out completely, releasing your intention out into the Universe.

Healing Fire

You will need:

- A picture of yourself
- Three blue candles
- Three purple candles

Get yourself and your altar ready with the items and then cast your circle. Set the candles in a circle around your picture. Hovering your hand over one of the candles, say: "I charge you by the powers of East, South, West, and North. I charge you by the powers of the Earth, Air, Fire, and Water. I charge you by the powers of the Sun, the Moon, and the Stars. Heal me of this (insert problem), its causes, and its manifestations. So, mote it be."

Do this with each of your candles. Then go through and start to light the candles in the same order that you charged them. When you light one, say, "Burn the sickness in your flame, burn the sickness that would maim. Burn the illness by your might, burn the illness in your light. Heal me of illness and pain and heal me of all that is bane. Heal me and set me free, with my will, so mote it be." Do this with each of the candles.

Once the candles are lit, sit quietly for a while and let them burn. Once you feel you have sat with them long enough, thank whatever deities you invited in and the elements and close your circle. Let the candles continue to burn until they go out.

Herbal Magic

This type of magic tends to smell really good, and herbs can infuse your magic with their properties.

Love Charm

You will need:

- A pink candle
- A small bowl
- One tablespoon of rose petals
- ¼ cup of chamomile flowers
- A teaspoon of St. John's wort
- A teaspoon of lemon balm
- A teaspoon of dried mugwort
- Six whole cloves

Gather all of these ingredients together and place them on your altar. Cast your circle and call in any deities that you want. Light your candle and then sit and take a couple of deep breaths to help calm the mind.

Add the chamomile, St. John's wort, lemon balm, and mugwort to the bowl and carefully mix them together with your fingers. Pour this into a small drawstring bag. Add in the cloves and then the rose petals. Pull the strings of the bag to close it.

Hold the bag in your hands, then close your eyes. Picture your entire body filled with white light, starting at your heart and then spreading all through your body. Once you have held this picture for a bit, let a soft pink light start to release from your heart and mix with the white light. As you picture this, say:

"As below, so above, I release all unseen blocks of love. As above, so below, my healed heart allows love to flow."

Let the candle burn out. Make sure that you keep your bag with you as much as you can. Once you feel that its energy has done what it can, bury the charm, or sprinkle the contents out onto the ground.

Business Luck

You will need:

- A piece of parchment
- Three gold coins
- A green ribbon
- A handful of bay leaves

Crumble up the parchment so that it is easy to move then flatten it back out. Lay the coins and bay leaves in the middle. Fold all four edges over and then tie the pack closed with the ribbon. You will use this as your charm for business luck.

Sit your right index finger on the package, then let your eyes fall closed. Take five minutes to meditate and visualize your goals for your business. Place the package in your office somewhere. Keep it safe and hidden, and it will bring you luck.

Protection Pouch

You will need:

- Sage oil
- A black candle
- Lavender buds
- Lavender oil
- Dried rose petals
- Dried thyme

- Black Obsidian
- Dried sage leaves
- A black piece of ribbon
- A black piece of square fabric

Start by casting your circle and meditating for a moment to get into a clear state of mind. Then anoint your candle with some of the sage oil. You can then press some of the thyme and sage into the candle.

Light the candle and picture yourself being cleansed and completely protected. Wave all of your other materials through the smoke of the candle to cleanse them. As you do this, say the following:

"Cleanse my soul, I ask of thee, cleanse my soul of all negativity, deeds, thoughts, wishes, and energy. Cleanse them all, so mote it is. And as you cleanse, protect my soul too, through day and night, and the morning dew. Protect from harm and negativity, cleanse it now, and leave only purity. It is done."

Say this three times. Once you have cleansed all of the parts of the pouch, blow the candle out. Place everything onto the piece of fabric and then pull the fabric around it and tie it closed with the ribbon.

Do this every single day until the candle has completely burned in order to improve the power. Bury the leftover wax in the earth. The pouch should be kept with you. If you feel that it needs an energy boost, then repeat this process.

Sleep Spell

You will need:

- A piece of parchment
- Smoky quartz
- Lavender sprigs

Get your bedroom ready by putting fresh sheets on your bed, dim the lights, and make sure the room is quiet. Get into a comfortable position on your bed and hold onto the quartz. Take a few moments to focus on the energy of the crystal and allow all of your troubling thoughts to drift away. When you feel calm, allow your eyes to close and say the mantra three times while you keep your stone in your right hand and move your wrist in clockwise circles.

"The moon is up, I hold its piece, the silver dust will guard my peace."

Take the piece of parchment and wrap it around the stone and lavender sprig. Lay this next to your bed. Now lay back and go to sleep.

Honey Jar Love Spell

You will need:

- A pink candle
- Pen and paper
- A mixture of dried violet, nutmeg, lavender, jasmine, bay leaves, basil, vanilla bean, red pepper, cinnamon, and cardamom (you don't have to use all of them)
- Pens or paints to decorate your jar
- Honey
- A jar

First off, make sure that your jar is clean. Then you can start to decorate the outside of the jar. Use colors like red and pink that represent love. You can write words or draw symbols that mean love to you.

Then take your pen and paper and write this down:

"With this spell, I attract to me, the person with whom I am meant to be. With this spell I cast tonight, love will come that for me is right."

Put the paper inside of the jar and then add your chosen flowers, roots, or herbs. Then pour in the honey. Sit the pink candle on the jar and light it. Sit the honey jar in a private spot in your home. You can recharge this by putting another candle over the jar and light. You can also do this with a tealight.

Color Magic

Color magic is something that you will see a lot of in witchcraft. Colors correspond with different energies, so you must match up colors with the purpose of your spell. This is used a lot with candle magic:

- **Black** – grounding, protection, safety, repelling black magic, banishing, pride, defense
- **Blue** – communication, water, sincerity, patience, truth, fidelity, good fortune
- **Brown** – food, earth, finding lost things, stability, concentration, house blessing
- **Copper** – passion, career growth, fertility
- **Gold** – luxury, masculine divinity, abundance, divination, prosperity, positivity
- **Green** – counteract jealousy, plant magic, weather, luck, healing, money, abundance, marriage
- **Indigo** – ambition, divination, psychic ability
- **Lavender** – intuition, knowledge
- **Light blue** – protection, peace, tranquility, spirituality
- **Orange** – investments, action, fun, ambition, joy, overcoming addiction, self-expression, creativity
- **Pink** – maturity, domestic harmony, healing, femininity, romance, friendship, love

- **Purple** – independence, change luck, contact spirits, influence, wisdom
- **Red** – competition, independence, sports, fire, action, sexual potency, courage, fertility, passion
- **Silver** – gambling luck, moon, meditation, intuition, stability
- **Violet** – tension, clarity, insight, goddess, spirituality
- **White** – all-purpose, cleansing
- **Yellow** – flexibility, air, confidence, inspiration, persuasion, memory, happiness, success, pleasure

Healing a Broken Heart

You will need:

- Honey
- Rose oil
- Lemon balm tea
- Rose petals
- A pink candle
- An egg

Sit in a place where you can be alone and undisturbed and hold the egg in your hand. Start thinking about the relationship that has ended, and all of the negativity you have about it. Let yourself feel it, and do not fight it off. Cry if you must. You should not be ashamed of releasing your feelings.

As you do this, roll the egg carefully over your face. Picture the egg soaking up all of the negative feelings. Project all of your unhappiness into the egg, treating it like a sponge soaking everything up. Once you feel like it has removed all of the negative feelings, take it outside and bury it. The earth will absorb all of your depression.

Go back inside and make yourself some lemon balm tea and sprinkle the rose petals in it. Add a bit of honey. Sit the candle before you and put some rose petals around it. Light it, and picture the smell of the roses and the candle's warmth mingling together and filling your body with its beauty and sweet scent. Allow yourself to be filled with warmth and comfort.

Improving Psychic Abilities

You will need:

- A notebook
- Jasmine or frankincense incense
- A white candle
- Four purple candles

You should aim to do this during a full or waxing moon.

Cast your circle and ground yourself. Sit the purple candles around you at the four cardinal points. Light your incense and sit the remaining candle in before you. Light the candles and then gaze at the flame of the white candle and clear your mind.

Picture your third eye taking in all of the energy from the white candle. Say:

"Vision of future present and past, a psychic spirit I do cast, to hear the unheard and see the unseen, psychic powers strong and keen. I open to see all with my third eye, psychic bonds to me I wish to tie. Unbind my spirit and my mind, so that my visions shall no longer be confined. Let my visions and dreams come before the rising sun, as I cast let my will be done, psychic powers I invoke thee. It is done, so mote it be."

After you have said this, blow the candles out and then close your circle. Pick up your notebook and walk to your bed. Begin to write down any messages that come to you while you sleep. They may seem cryptic to begin with, but you will start to understand things.

Crystal Magic

Love Spell to Attract a Specific Person

You will need:

- Rose quartz
- Four red candles
- A red pen
- A square piece of paper
- A cauldron

This should be done at night. Begin by casting your circle, placing the red candles at the four cardinal points to mark your circle. Start a fire in your cauldron and like the candles. On the paper, with the red pen, draw a heart. Then write the person's name in the center. Pick up the rose quartz and gaze upon the paper as you picture pink energy emanating from the crystal, into your heart, and then down onto the paper. Let all of the love you have for that person pour into this moment.

Kiss the paper three times. Place it in the fire and let it burn. Say three times:

"My heart ablaze and shining, this love I do send to thee. If you find a place in your heart to love me, by the greatest good, so mote it be."

Now you can close the circle. Try to keep the rose quartz close to you for at least a month.

Career Success

You will need:

- An offering bowl
- Money
- Two green fluorite crystals
- Ten bay leaves
- Amber incense
- Essential oil for your zodiac sign
- Four green candles
- A white candle
- A photo of yourself

Make sure you are wearing white when you do this. Wash your hands and apply some of the essential oil on them. Sit the green candles at North, South, East, and West. Set the white candle before you. The incense should be to the left of the white candle. Sit the money, fluorite, and bay leaves in the bowl and set it to the right.

Set your picture in front of the white candle.

Center and ground yourself, and then cast your circle and light the green candles, and then the white. Pick up the white candle to light your incense.

Drop some of the white candle incense on your photo. Pick up the offering bowl, holding it in both hands, and really focus yourself on your picture. Say three times:

"Success is coming soon to me. Prosperity is flowing unto me. So, mote it be."

Sit quietly for a bit and picture having financial abundance. Money is coming to you easily. You are in alignment with abundance. Picture what this means. Allow yourself to be immersed in what this feels like. The longer you can picture this, the better it will be.

Once you feel you have sat long enough, blow out all of the candles, making sure the white one is last. Close your circle and allow the incense to finished burning.

Rituals

Rituals, as you have learned, play a big part in Pagan religions. From the Sabbats during the year to the Esbats at every full moon, rituals are important for Pagans. Through rituals, Pagans connect themselves to nature, celebrate life, make magic, and create community. Rituals help them to deepen their relationship with the Divine in many different forms. Pagans evolve and flourish through rituals.

Rituals can be elaborate or simple. One person or many people can do them. Some require much planning, while others tend to be spontaneous. Rituals can be a theatrical and scripted performance done by a few and observed by the rest. Some are improvisational interactive. Some Pagan paths have rituals that have become the standard and are repeatedly done. Some rites have evolved. Rituals can be long or short and can last several days.

Some of them are completely silent, while others involve drumming, singing, and cheering. Most have a moderate mixture of sounds and silent meditation. Most rituals are colorful and will include different tools like cauldrons, crystals, pentacles, chalices, incense, and wands. Many people have specific clothing that they wear during rituals like special jewelry, necklaces, garland crowns, capes, and robes. Some have naked rituals or wear body paint.

Some rituals will require dancing or some ritual gestures. However, some are all done through imagery and visualized in the mind. Rituals can take place during the day, at night, and throughout the year. Rituals are often held on each Sabbat. Some Pagans perform daily rites like meal blessings, greeting the night, greeting the day, and dream incubation. Many Pagans hold a ritual on their birthday and for other special occasions.

Rituals are also sometimes helped at life passages like birth, enhance fertility, bless pregnancy, aid in conception, and facilitate birthing. Furthermore, coming of age rituals are popular. There are many different types of rituals, and you can choose what areas of your life that you want to celebrate.

First on the ritual list for this chapter are the Esbats.

Esbats

Esbats are fairly new rituals that came about with neopaganism, so these are probably not something that your ancestors celebrated. Then again, the Moon has always played a big part in Paganism, so they may have had their own version of Esbats.

Esbats are typically rituals to celebrate the Goddess during the full moon. Some people will celebrate Esbats on the new moon. You can do whichever feels right to you. Each year has thirteen Esbats. The full moon is celebrated because it represents fertility, the pregnant Mother Earth, and honors the Goddess. Esbats are normally celebrated through magical works, singing, dancing, and then followed with cakes and wine. Some people will evoke the Goddess and read poems to honor her.

In the witch's life, the Moon should not occupy a lesser purpose than the Sun, and trying to force the Moon's cycles to match up the cycles of the Sun is confusing as well as against nature. It forces the energy of the Moon to be at the mercy of the energy of the Sun.

Worshipping under the light of the moon has been an ancient practice, one that motivates our primitive centers and pulls into the spell of the Moon. While there is evidence of Yule dating back 12,000 years, evidence of lunar calendars goes back 40,000 years, making them the oldest ritual.

The reason the Moon is most often connected to the Goddess is because of the connection with the menstrual cycle. Over 29 days, the Moon appears to mimic the cycle of death and rebirth, and because birth is viewed as a feminine function, the Moon thus became a symbol of femininity.

Christianity did not originate the idea of a three-in-one god. The phases of the Moon are connected with the woman's three phases of life: virgin, mother, and crone. When waxing, the Goddess is the virgin. She is sexual, adventurous, and traverses all worlds. When full, she is the nurturing mother, strong, protective, and powerful. When waning, she is the crone, the grandmother with all of her no-nonsense ways, wisdom, and wit. Through rituals, we honor these aspects.

Many solitary witches will take advantage of this fact and celebrate the Moon in both the full and new phases. Due to life, covens will often just celebrate one or the other.

If you choose to celebrate a new moon Esbat, it gives you the chance to worship the darker parts of your craft. This does not mean negative or evil aspects. The dark aspect is just the parts that are hidden, the shadow instead of the light, and it reflects our inner being much like the Sun reflects the outer self.

If you choose to celebrate a full moon Esbat, it is often a frenetic, ribald celebration. This is suitable for "lunatics" who were thought to display their insanity when the Moon was full.

Magic for any need is performed during these rituals, both by solitary practitioners and covens. Spells for gain are typically done during the waxing phase. And spells for loss are typically done during the waning phase. The full moon is often used for spells for love, psychic enhancement, families, mothers, children, and wholeness.

Drawing down the Moon is the most common ritual that is done during an Esbat, along with the ceremony of cakes and ale.

Drawing Down the Moon

This version of the ritual is made for the solitary witch, but it can easily be done in a coven setting, as well. This is also not a spell for beginners; it is a very advanced form of magic that requires a lot of skill. This is an act of divine possession. You have to reach a deep trance and willingly offer yourself to the Goddess. It won't work if you are not ready. So, when you do this for the first time, do not expect anything to happen. As you practice and learn more about your craft, it will become more powerful. Even if you are advanced, sometimes the effects of this will be subtle.

What you need:

- Full moon incense – optional
- Goddess attire – optional
- A Book of shadows or journal
- An offering or libation
- A white candle
- A moonstone
- A selenite crystal

This should be done during the full moon, and if you can, do it outside. However, if you do not have a private place outside to do this, then it is better to stay inside. The ritual won't work too well if you are worried that somebody will see you.

Before you begin, prepare yourself. A week before the full moon, meditate each day, eat as clean as possible, and provide the Goddess with daily offerings. The day before, perform a purification bath. The night of, wear your goddess clothes, if you use them, or get into comfortable ritual clothing. Having goddess robes can help reinforce your connection. The goal is to make sure that you have the right mindset.

Once you feel ready, gather your tools and set up your altar. Get the space ready by purifying it and then ground yourself. Cast your circle in your chosen way.

Light the candle and incense. Grasp the selenite in your non-dominant hand and the moonstone in your dominant hand. Raise your arms and hands high into a Y position with your palms facing up. This is what is known as the Goddess pose.

Then you need to invoke the Goddess. You can do this by saying: "I invoke thee and call upon the mighty Mother of us all. Bringer of fruitfulness by seeds and by root. I invoke thee by stem and bud. I invoke thee by life and love and call upon thee to descend into the body of this thy priestess and servant."

You can also chant a Goddess mantra. Just do whatever feels natural to you. Now, stand quietly for a few moments. You should start to feel a rush of energy. Let the Goddess' energy fill you. Surrender yourself to it. Use all of your senses to feel the energy. If you feel like you need to say or do something, then do it. Do not hesitate because this is the Goddess working through you.

Once you feel the energy is fading, express your gratitude, and offer her something. You can then progress with the rest of your Esbat ritual and then journal your experience. Free the Goddess by closing your circle and snuffing out the candle. Then you need to ground yourself—drinking or eating is the best option.

This ritual can sometimes leave behind side effects. You may be more emotional for a few days. You might notice that your chakras are tingling, or you could have vivid dreams. You should often journal about these things, and do not worry—this will start to fade.

Cakes and Ale

This ritual normally concludes Esbats rituals and is done with solitary practitioners and in covens. It is probably one of the easiest rituals you can do. This might be a good place to start when it comes to Esbat rituals until you become experienced in drawing down the moon. For this, you do not have to use alcoholic beverages or cake. They are both flexible and can be substituted.

You will need:

- Bread or cake
- Wine, ale, water, or juice

The bread and wine are symbolic of the Goddess and the blood of her womb. It does not matter what specific deity you worship, either. Prepare your altar and place the bread and drink in the center. Pick up the bread and hold it before you, like you were giving it to somebody. Say a blessing that focuses on the Goddess gifting your bread, instead of blessing the actual bread. You could say:

"Blessed by the Goddess who gives herself to us in the form of a bountiful harvest. Blessed be her bread, the gift of her body that sustains and nurtures us. By all that is sacred, so mote it be."

Break part of the bread off and eat it. If you are in a group setting, pass the bread around clockwise, and everybody will take a piece and eat. Next, you will pick up the cup, like you are offering it. You then say a similar blessing:

"Blessed be the womb of the Goddess in whose blood we are formed and from which we are born. Blessed be her gift of drink, which links us to her powers of creation. From her womb, we came, and to it, we shall one day return to await rebirth. By all that is sacred, so mote it be."

Take a sip of the drink, and if there is more than one person, pass it around until everybody has taken a sip. Once the cup has made it back around to you, pour the remaining liquid outside and place the rest of the bread on top of it. This is an offering to the Goddess, and the bread is something that animals can eat.

Self-Dedication Ritual

Most people often choose to take a solitary path because it is sometimes hard to find a coven for many reasons. It could be that you cannot find one that aligns with your beliefs and ethics, or there aren't many where you live. Some covens do not "advertise" because you have to be brought in by other members. Covens like to keep things secretive, and we all know why. However, one thing that covens do for new members that solitary witches do not always get is a dedication rite. But the good news is that this book will show you how to do your own dedication ritual.

In a coven, there is a formal ceremony to initiate new members into the group. The person will dedicate themselves to the group and the group's gods and goddesses. They are typically initiated by the High Priest or Priestess.

So, what does it mean to self-dedicate? Many people believe that you have to study for a year and a day before they will do their self-dedication. However, you do not have to do this.

You could choose to wait until the phase of the new moon because this is the time for new beginnings. You need to remember that a self-dedication is a commitment. You should not do this for fun, at random, or without some significant thought.

The goals of this ritual are to bring you closer to the Divine so that you can declare your connection with your path. This is a fairly important step along your journey, so you should probably include things that make the rite more official and formal in practice and feel.

For example, you could perform a ritual bath before you begin. You can also use some altar tools that you have made yourself, but you don't have to. When you do, though, it makes the ritual more unique and personal. Some will choose a new magical name so that you can take the time to introduce yourself to your chosen god and goddess during the dedication. If you have a great memory, you can memorize some ritual blessing beforehand. Do not worry though; you can copy it down into your Book of Shadows just in case you forget.

You will need:

- A white candle
- Salt
- Blessing oil

Now, remember: This is just a suggestion or template that you can adapt to your needs and traditions. If at all possible, do this skyclad—meaning you wear nothing. Find a place that is free of distractions, quiet, and private. Send your kids out and turn your phone off. Start by grounding yourself. Reach your inner peace, and allow yourself to become relaxed. Push away all of the mundane life distractions, like bills, work, etc. Focus fully on you and tranquility.

Now, sprinkle some salt on the ground or floor and stand on it. Light the candle and feel the flame's warmth. Gaze into its glow and think about all of the goals that you have for your spiritual self. Think about what is motivating you to do this self-dedication. Standing in front of your altar, say:

"I am the child of the God and Goddess, and I ask them to bless me."

Dip one finger into the blessing oil, and close your eyes. Anoint your forehead by tracing a pentagram on it. Say:

"May my mind be blessed, so that I can accept the wisdom of the God and Goddess."

Then move down and anoint your eyelids. Be very careful and do not get the oil in your eyes. Say:

"May my eyes be blessed, so I can see my way clearly upon this path."

Then anoint your nose. Say:

"May my nose be blessed, so I can breathe in the essence of all that is Divine."

Then anoint your lips. Say:

"May my lips be blessed, so I may always speak with honor and respect."

Then move to your chest and anoint it. Say:

"May my heart be blessed, so I may love and be loved."

Then anoint the tops of the hands. Say:

"May my hands be blessed, so that I may use them to heal and help others."

Next, anoint the genital areas, again being careful. Say:

"May my womb be blessed, so that I may honor the creation of life." Men will need to change this to work for them.

Then anoint the bottom of your feet. Say:

"May my feet be blessed, so that I may walk side by side with the Divine."

If you have chosen specific deities to worship, pledge your loyalty now. If you do not have specific ones, you can say, "Mother and Father," or "God and Goddess." Say:

"Tonight, I pledge my dedication to the God and Goddess. I will walk with them beside me, and ask them to guide me on this journey. I pledge to honor them and ask that they allow me to grow closer to them. As I will, so it shall be."

Then take a few minutes to meditate. Feel the power of the ritual, and fell the God and Goddess' energy around you. You have now connected yourself with the Divine, who will be watching over you.

Birth Rituals

Many cultures have their own birth rites, many of which involve presenting the newborn to the family's gods. While the God and Goddess have probably been aware of the new arrival, it is always a good idea to perform a formal presentation. A birth rite joins the child to the Earth and heavens. This should be done as soon after the birth as possible so that the child can start to form a relationship with the God and Goddess. You can do the same thing if you adopt a child as well.

You can either do this as a family ceremony, or you can invite other friends and family as well. Pick whichever works best for the needs of your family. Ideally, this should be done when you first bring the baby home before you walk inside, but you can do it whenever the family feels up to it.

Stand outside of the front door, holding the baby. The people who are present should hold hands and surround the person with the baby. Say:

"God and Goddess of our home, God and Goddess of our hearth, today we present you with someone new. (He or She) is a member of our family, and this is (his/her) new home. We ask you to welcome (him/her), we ask you to love (him/her), we ask you to protect (him/her), we ask you to bless (him/her)."

You should have a cup of milk, water, or wine at the door. Before you walk in, pass the cup around the group. Each time a person takes a drink, they should say, "Welcome, baby, to our home. May the God and Goddess love you as much as we do."

When everybody has taken a sip, touch a drop of the liquid on the baby's lips. You may now walk inside. Travel to the family's altar.

Everybody should hold hands and surround the person with the baby. Say:

"God and Goddess of our home, God and Goddess of our hearth, today we present you with someone new. (He or She) is a member of our family, and this is (his/her) new home. Watch over (him/her) as (he/she) grows. Watch over (him/her) as (he/she) lives. Watch over (him/her) with love."

The cup should make another trip around the group, and place one more drop on the baby's lips. Place the cup on the altar where it should stay overnight. The next morning, walk the cup out the front door and then pour the rest of the liquid on the ground.

Birthday Ritual

Birthdays are a big deal, and no matter how old we are, we should still celebrate them. For children, they typically have their own ritual every year in the form of a birthday party. However, due to society, as we age, we are supposed to give up those parties and let our birthday pass like any other day. But birthdays are special, so we should make them special. This is a simple and easy way to celebrate your birthday and bless your following year.

All you will need is a white candle.

On your birthday, light the candle and say the following blessing.

"This candle burns for birthday blessings. In golden light, good luck finds a spark. By candle flame, my fortune rises. Enrich my life with friendship's mark. Bright candle keeps me safe and healthy. Give pleasure by both day and night. I blow your flames for this year's wishes and pinch your wick for future bright. The bright candle shines upon my birthday, abundance flow from heaven to Earth, grant me romance, wealth, and wisdom. So, mote it be my day of birth."

Croning Celebration

Crone used to be used as an insult. It implied that the woman in question was unloved, unwanted, and ugly. Women of advanced age were shunned as useless, and there was not anything more to be celebrated. Fortunately, things are very different.

The female elder used to be considered the wise woman. She shared her knowledge, healed, and taught others. She helped work through disputes and influenced the tribal leaders, and she took care of the dying as they spent their last minutes on Earth. For most women in Pagan religions, reaching the life phase of the Crone is an important milestone. Women are now postively reclaiming the name of Crone.

Croning ceremonies normally do not take place until a woman has reached at least 50. Some traditions suggest waiting until after menopause to move into the Crone phase. However, some women in their 30s have stopped having their periods, and some women continue to menstruate well into their 60s, so you can time your ceremony to whatever works for you.

There are no set rules on how to perform a Croning ceremony. Sometimes, in covens, it is led by a High Priestess; in other cases, it is performed by a woman who has already reached the position of Crone. These ceremonies tend to be done as part of a women's circle. However, you can do whatever feels right to you. Most ceremonies will include the following:

- A ritual cleansing or bath
- Chanting and singing
- A guided meditation to honor the Wise Woman
- Tools: crown, garland, special cloak
- Poetry, music, or drumming to celebrate womanhood

- An altar set up with pictures of other female relatives and friends that the Crone finds empowering
- A celebratory meal
- A symbol of passing into the Cronehood, like crossing a threshold
- The exchange of blessings or gifts

Some women decide to take on a new name during their Croning ceremony; this is mandatory, but people tend to take on different names during other milestones, so it is something that you could do. Your Crone name can be something that only you know, or it could be something that you announce to everybody.

Reaching Cronehood is a major life event. It is a celebration of everything that you have learned and what is to come. For many, it is time to create brand-new commitments.

Creating Your Own Ritual

There are many things in life that you might want to celebrate with a ritual. While you can find lots of rituals online and in other books, you may want to come up with your own. You might discover, in coming up with your own ritual, it will help you to follow the same type of format every time. After all, the main part of a ritual is the idea of repetition. This does not mean that you must say the same words, but you can keep the same general order of things, and it can help you to tune into the process.

Rituals are also mean to be celebratory. This means that you need to have something to celebrate. This can be any phase in a person's life, the change of a season, the phase of the Moon, or a Sabbat. You can celebrate anything and everything, but you need to know what you are celebrating so that you know how to focus your ritual.

You should answer the following questions. They will help guide you when it comes to creating your ritual:

• *Why do you want to have a ritual? What is the point of it? What do you want to celebrate?* There could be several purposes for the ritual, or just one. But you want to be clear on this.

• *Who is going to be involved? Are you going to do this in a coven, with some friends, or alone? Is one person leading while everybody watches, or will others be participating? Is this going to be public or private?*

• *Do you need to come up with a sacred space? Are you going to need to cast a circle, or just simple smudge the area?*

• *Do you need to call upon a certain deity?*

In most traditions, the idea of centering and grounding, and raising energy and mediation is an important part of rituals. It is mainly up to you as to how you will perform your ceremony based on your needs or the needs of a group. Here is how a ritual could be run:

1. Everybody who is participating is welcomed into the sacred space one at a time and blessed. If you are doing a solitary ritual, this isn't necessary.

2. Call the quarters or cast your circle.

3. Perform a mediation session.

4. Call upon specific deities and make offerings.

5. A ritual to celebrate whatever it is that you are celebrating.

6. Perform any additional energy work or healing.

7. Close the circle.

8. Celebrate with some refreshments.

Of course, this is just an example. It can take a more informal approach, as well. It all depends on what you want to celebrate. If you are doing a group ritual, and you want other people to

participate, make sure that they know what they are going to be doing. The further ahead you plan the ritual, the better it will be because you will be more prepared. Above all else, just have fun.

Spells

Space Cleansing Ritual

Cleansing your space before performing any spell is one of the most important things you can do. You can begin any spell with this ritual, or you can do this when you feel a room is feeling stale and stagnant.

You will need:

- Sage incense
- A red taper
- A blue taper
- A brown taper
- A yellow taper
- A white taper
- A silver taper
- A chalice of water
- A broom

Gather all of your things and place them on your altar. Drape a black cloth over them until they need to be used. Choose a time a date to perform this; the new moon is the best time.

The area that you are cleansing should be cleaned thoroughly. This means washing the walls and floors, vacuuming, and so on. Take a bath or shower and picture all types of debris being cleansed from you and let yourself feel completely clean.

When you feel ready, remove the black cloth and place the yellow candle at the East, red at the South, blue at the West, and brown at the North to mark your circle. Sit the silver and white candles on your altar. Light the incense.

Stand in front of your altar. Take a deep breath in and then light the white candle. Walk around the room in a clockwise motion and light each element candle. Take your broom and sweep a circle as you walk clockwise inside of the circle. Say:

"Sweep, sweep, sweep this place by powers of Air, I cleanse this space."

Take a moment to close your eyes and picture Air moving throughout this space. Go back to the altar and take the silver candle. With the white, light the silver one. Take another clockwise walk around the circle. Say:

"Light, light, I light this space. By the powers of Fire, I cleanse this space."

Picture the energy of Fire cleansing the circle. Go back to the altar and pick up your chalice of water. Walk clockwise around the circle again and sprinkle the water around with your right hand. Say:

"Liquid, liquid, I wash this place. By powers of Water, I cleanse this space."

Feel the energy of Water flowing around the circle. Go back to the altar and pick up your bowl of dirt. Walk around the circle, clockwise, sprinkle some dirt. Say:

"Dirt, dirt as I walk this place, by powers of Earth, I cleanse this space."

Really feel the Earth cleansing your circle. Place the bowl back on the altar. While in the Goddess position, say:

"I now direct the energy of the Universe to forever fill and bless this place."

Really feel the energy of your body mix with the Universe. Once it feels like the energy starts to dissipate, go back to your altar and place your hands on the altar, say:

"This altar is dedicated to the Lord and Lady of Light. May it serve me well."

If you do not need to cleanse any tools right now, you can end everything by thanking the God and Goddess and elements. Ground yourself by placing your hands on the floor and feel everything drain back into the Earth. Move your right hand overhead in a counter-clockwise way, and then circle the room. Say:

"This circle is open, may it never be broken."

Fertility Spell

This spell can help a woman get pregnant, and it should be done during ovulation for the greatest effect.

You will need:

- A boline
- An agate crystal
- A banana
- An apple

Wash the banana and apple. Cut them up and mix them in a bowl. Take the agate and bowl of fruit outside. Use your garden (if you have one), or use a forest or park. If you can, find a birch tree; otherwise, just pick a healthy tree, which is calling you in.

If you can, cast your circle, or sit and picture a protective shield. Call up the God and Goddess. Let them know that you want to conceive. You can say this out loud or within your mind. Let them know about the future family you want and how you want to become a mom. Tell them how you would show your child and your family love. Be honest and speak openly. Pick up the bowl of fruit, say:

"God and Goddess of fertility and fruition, please accept this offering. In return for my blessed child to come to be, all be well. So, mote it be."

Place the fruit at the roots of the tree. Pick up the agate and move into a place of joy, trust, and love. Picture the way it would feel to have a child growing within you. Know that as long as you expect the best and hold a positive focus, the best is going to come. Picture your child already here. What do they look like? What is it like to be caring for your baby? What is life like later on? Picture all of the big life events for your child. Let yourself go into a deep visualization as you hold onto the agate and charge it with all of the joy from your visualization.

Stay here and meditate for as long as you can. Once you are done, thank the elements and the God and Goddess. Keep your agate with you. Hold the stone whenever you need a reminder.

Money Carpet Spell

This spell will help you attract money into your life.

You will need:

- Basil
- Baking soda

You do not need a circle for this. Mix the baking soda and basil and sprinkle it throughout your house before you vacuum. Then vacuum your house. This will help to increase the flow of money in your home.

Protection Spell

This protection spell acts as an electric fence around your house. It will keep out any evil that wants to harm you.

You will need:

- Four quartz

All you need to do is bury one quartz at each corner of your property line. This will keep anybody with any ill-will away from your home.

Good Luck

This spell can help you bring luck into your life.

You will need:

- Allspice

You can begin by casting a circle if you want to make this formal, but you don't have to. All you need to do is take some whole allspice and burn it. You can try just to light it, but it might be best to use a charcoal disk, light it, and then place the allspice on top of it. Burning the allspice in your home will help to draw in luck, money, and speed healing.

Love Spell

This particular love spell can only be done if you know the person that you want to attract as a partner.

You will need:

- An apple

This is extremely easy. Slice the apple in half. Give one of the halves to the person you would like to attract and eat the other half yourself. This will ensure a loving and prosperous relationship.

Money Jar

This is another magic spell and is done in a jar. It is very simple, and you likely have most of the ingredients already on hand.

You will need:

- Five pecans
- Five whole allspice
- Five cloves
- Five cinnamon sticks
- Five sesame seeds
- Five kernels of dried wheat
- Five kernels of dried corn
- Five quarters
- Five dimes
- Five pennies

Get a tall thin bottle and place all of the listed items into the bottle. Place the cap on and make sure it is closed tightly. Using your dominant hand, shake the bottle for five minutes as you say the following:

"Herbs and silver, copper and grain, work to increase my money gain."

Set the bottle down on a table somewhere in your home. Keep your wallet, pocketbook, purse, or checkbook near the bottle whenever you are home. Let the money come into your life.

Wish Spell

This is a simple spell to share what it is that you want in life with the Universe.

You will need:

- A piece of paper that represents your wish
- A candle that represents you

When you are ready to do this spell, start by casting your circle. Light your candle. Take the paper, and on one side of it, draw a pentacle. Flip it over, and then write out what it is that you desire or wish to come true. Place the paper in the flame of the candle and let it catch on fire. Allow the paper to burn, and as it does so, focus on what your wish is. Let the paper rest on a safe surface where it can burn without burning you or your house.

As the paper continues to burn, say, "May this candle represent thee, as I place this desire in the flame shall my need be seen. Fulfill my need as quick as can be by the power of three bring the need to me, so mote it be."

Let the candle burn out and bury the ashes. Close your circle once you are done.

Peace of Mind

You will need:

- Jasmine incense
- A lavender candle

If you feel you need to, or you want to, begin by casting a circle. Then light your candle and incense. As you stand in front of your altar, say the following:

"Worries be gone, I need you not more. Worries are gone, out of my door. Stress, strains, worry, and strife leave me now and be gone from my life. As I will it, so mote it be."

Sit in meditation for a while after this. Allow your mind to relax and feel all of your worries being lifted away and released.

Conclusion

Thank you for making it through to the end of this book. It should have been informative and provided you with all of the tools you need to achieve your witchcraft goals, whatever they might be.

You should now have a pretty good understanding of what witchcraft is, along with Wicca and Paganism. They are not some evil, devil-worshipping religions that the people of the Christian faith have tried to make them out to be. They are simple nature religions that bring a person close to Earth and to themselves. If you so feel compelled, start trying out some of the spells, but make sure you have a clear intention in mind. Above all else, follow your heart.

Finally, if you found this book useful in any way, a review on Amazon is always appreciated!

Check out another book by Amy Golden

Made in the USA
San Bernardino, CA
14 January 2020